# A PASSION FOR GOD

PRAYERS AND MEDITATIONS
ON THE BOOK OF ROMANS

with a New Paraphrase by

*Raymond C. Ortlund, Jr.*

CROSSWAY BOOKS • WHEATON, ILLINOIS
A DIVISION OF GOOD NEWS PUBLISHERS

Art Direction/Design: Mark Schramm

First printing 1994

Printed in the United States of America

"To eat, to breathe" by Francis Schaeffer, © 1960 *Christianity Today.* Used
by permission.

**Library of Congress Cataloging-in-Publication Data**
Ortlund, Raymond C., Jr.
  A passion for God / Raymond C. Ortlund, Jr.
    p.   cm.
Includes bibliographical references.
    1. Bible. N.T.—Devotional literature.  2. Bible N.T. Romans—
Paraphrases, English.  I. Title.
BS2665.4.0786 1994    227'.1077—dc20        93-38010
ISBN 0-89107-765-0

| 03 | 02 | 01 | 00 | 99 | 98 | 97 | 96 | 95 | 94 |
|----|----|----|----|----|----|----|----|----|----|
| 15 | 14 | 13 | 12 | 11 | 10 | 9 | 8 | 7 | 6 | 5 | 4 | 3 | 2 | 1 |

For three friends
whose Bible - and prayer-saturated lives
greatly inspire me:

Hudson T. Armerding,
John Piper,
and my own father.

I love them.

# TABLE OF
# CONTENTS

# FOREWORD

FOUR DECADES AGO PLUS, I began my ministry in a small village in eastern Pennsylvania. Armed with seminary diploma and ordination certificate, the ink on each barely dry, Anne and I arrived at our first parish with three little people filling the backseat of our very old car: two little girls, ages three and two, and tiny Ray, Jr.

My heart was on fire. I had been told (by my mentor, Dr. Donald Grey Barnhouse), and I had also read, that the preaching of the truths of the book of Romans had preceded every major revival in church history. So I purposed to begin my ministry preaching Romans. Here, for instance, is what Frederick L. Godet, the nineteenth-century Swiss pastor and theologian, had written:

> When the Epistle to the Romans appeared for the first time, it was to the church a word in season. Every time that, in the course of the ages, it has recovered the place of honour which belongs to it, it has inaugurated a new era.[1]

And this further comment by Godet:

> The Reformation was undoubtedly the work of the Epistle to the Romans, as well as of that to the Galatians. And the probability is that every great spiritual revival in the church will be connected as effect and cause with a deeper understanding of this book.[2]

From my first Sunday I began preaching through Romans, as best I knew how. And an interesting thing happened. I was the one revived.

Ever since, I have had a deep heart-love for this book of Romans.

Paul called it "my gospel."

Luther called it "the clearest gospel of all."

Tyndale called it "a light and way into the whole of Scripture."

Coleridge called it "the profoundest book in existence."

Chrysostom had it read to him twice a week.

Melanchthon copied it twice in his own hand, to make it his very own.

And I have also had a deep heart-love for revival. It is the reason Anne and I serve under "Renewal Ministries" to this very day.

Our son, Ray, Jr., has this same burden for revival. May I say this about him? Indulge me. He has an unswerving commitment to the Word of God. And he has a passion for stating the gospel precisely, with understandable but accurate words. He and I have talked on the phone over the miles weekly, sharing our burden for revival in the church. When together, the two of us have knelt in prayer, weeping before God in our longings for Him to revisit His people with another awakening. This volume comes out of Ray's great love for the Bible and for the gospel and for the church.

As his mother and I have read the manuscript, we have shaken our heads and wondered, "Where did this man come from?" Obviously, the prayers stimulated by his own long hours of poring over Romans in the Greek text—these prayers show that God has been dealing with him deeply. And as I have read, God has dealt with me, too.

In this present day—this parched, lusterless, confused, sin-stained day—you and I need another humble, prayer-saturated exposure to God's great Epistle, which is not only to the Romans but also to us.

Raymond C. Ortlund, Sr.
Newport Beach, California
June 11, 1993

# PREFACE

THIS BOOK flows out of the two great passions energizing my life. The one is a passion for God. James 4:8 has marked me: "Draw near to God, and he will draw near to you." To commune with God by faith in deep personal fellowship is the highest fulfillment one can experience. I have tasted and seen that the Lord is good, and I want more.

My other passion is for Holy Scripture, the primary vehicle for bringing us near to God. It is perhaps expected that a seminary teacher will show a certain reserve or formality with the Bible, to maintain his professorial bearing. But I can't do that. I love the Bible. "The words that I speak to you, they are spirit and they are life," Jesus said in John 6:63. Spirit and life! What else is there worth having? And how else are they to be found, but through the Word of God?

Thomas Watson (ca. 1620-1686), the Puritan pastor, brings these two passions together with wise simplicity. After quoting Deuteronomy 6:5—"Love the Lord your God with all your heart and with all your soul and with all your strength"—Watson continues:

> *What is love? It is a holy fire kindled in the affections, whereby a Christian is carried out strongly after God as the supreme good. What is the antecedent of love for God? The antecedent of love is knowledge. The Spirit shines upon the understanding and discovers*

> *the beauties of wisdom, holiness and mercy in God.*
> *These are the magnet to entice and draw out love for*
> *God. . . . If the sun be set in the understanding, there*
> *must be night in the affections.*[1]

When you look at your Bible, what do you see? I have learned to see the Bible as kindling for a holy fire. Scripture is meant to inform us, and thus to inflame us. It is meant to illuminate our thoughts of God, and thus to to ignite our affections for God. So in our personal Bible study, as we strive to think and learn, we are gathering kindling for devotion and worship in our hearts. And even more, we are amassing kindling for revival and reformation in the church.

Paul's letter to the Romans is of this explosive nature. Under the blessing of the Holy Spirit, it warms Christians with release from guilt, confidence in God and certainty in their faith. It ignites Christians with joy and moral courage. It fires Christians with energy for bold new ventures of holy obedience. Let me put it this way. The more you understand, believe and love Romans, the more filled you will be with God's Spirit, the more you will walk in newness of life and the more your life will count for the great cause of the gospel.

But why this particular approach—Scripture with prayer? Because every generation of Christians, and our own most urgently, needs to rediscover afresh both the truth of Holy Scripture and the nearness of God. More than new church growth strategies, more than political clout, more than anything else, we need to behold a new vision of God and to live in deep personal communion with him. What Moses urged upon Israel long ago holds no less for us today:

> *See, I have taught you decrees and laws as the Lord my*
> *God commanded me, so that you may follow them in*
> *the land you are entering to take possession of it.*

*Observe them carefully, for this will show your wisdom and understanding to the nations, who will hear about all these decrees and say, "Surely this great nation is a wise and understanding people." What other nation is so great as to have their gods near them the way the Lord our God is near us whenever we pray to him? And what other nation is so great as to have such righteous decrees and laws as this body of laws I am setting before you today?* (Deuteronomy 4:5-8)

Instead of being the target of talk-show jokes, the Christian church *could* amaze the world with two impressive qualities: her wisdom from God's Word, and the nearness of her God. We Christians have in the Bible a treasure that the modern world does not even believe exists, namely, Truth. And we also have a prayer-hearing God who is able to orchestrate events and transform our lives for his glory in the spiritual conflict engulfing the world today. There could be nothing more socially relevant than a new generation of Christians who know the Bible profoundly and who experience the reality of God daily in their souls. That will renew the church today, and this book is intended to contribute to that goal.

I wish to acknowledge my indebtedness to the many friends who have made a contribution to this book. Thanks are due to Don Carson, Jack Crabtree, Wayne Grudem, Murray Harris, Dave Howard, Jr., Bing Hunter, S. Lewis Johnson, Jr., Dennis Magary, Tom Nettles, Ken Orr, Iain Paton, Bob Perrone, Rob Rayburn, Bruce Ware, John Woodbridge; to Doug Moo, an expert on Romans, who not only allowed me to sit in on his Autumn, 1992 doctoral seminar on Romans 9-11 here at Trinity but also critiqued my rough draft and advised me wisely on its improvement; to Lane Dennis, Len Goss, Brian Ondracek, Chuck Phelps, Helen Durham and Ted Griffin at Crossway Books for their generous help; and not least to my wife Jan, the joy of my heart, and to my children, Eric, Krista, Dane and Gavin, who brighten my daily life with much laughter.

I consecrate this book to the greater glory of God, with the earnest prayer that he will revive and reform his church today through a Spirit-empowered rediscovery of the gospel. Thomas Scott (1747-1821), a nominal Christian turned radical by the power of the gospel, will speak for me as I bring this Preface to a close:

*And now, beloved reader, let me conclude with leaving it upon thy conscience to search for the truth of the gospel in the study of God's Word, accompanied by prayer, as thou wouldst search for hid treasure. I give thee this counsel, expecting to meet thee at the day of judgment, that our meeting may be with joy and not with grief. May the Lord incline thee to follow it with that solemn season in view! Time how short! Eternity how long! Life how precarious and vanishing! Death how certain! The pursuits and employments of this present life how vain, unsatisfying, trifling and vexatious! God's favor and eternal life how unspeakably precious! His wrath, the never-quenched fire, the never-dying worm, how dreadful! Oh! trifle not away the span of life in heaping up riches, which shortly must be left for ever, and which profit not in the day of wrath, in such pleasures and amusements as will issue in eternal torments, or in seeking that glory which shall be swallowed up in everlasting infamy. Agree with me but in this, that it is good to redeem precious time, to labor for the meat that endureth unto everlasting life, and to attend principally to the one thing needful. Take but thy measure of truth as well as duty from the Word of God. Be willing to be taught of God. Meditate on his Word day and night. Let it be "the light of thy feet and the lantern of thy paths."*[2]

# INTRODUCTION

AT THE HEART of this book, where its warmth and energy are generated, is the gospel of Jesus Christ as taught in Paul's letter to the Romans. My rendering of Romans, although based upon the Greek text, is not a translation. It is a fresh paraphrase of the argument of the epistle.[1] So what is the difference between a translation and this type of paraphrase? Let me illustrate. I would *translate* Romans 1:18 like this:

> For the wrath of God from heaven is revealed against all ungodliness and unrighteousness of men who suppress the truth in unrighteousness.

But my *paraphrase* expounds and amplifies the sense of Romans 1:18, in its contextual connection with Romans 1:17, like this:

> While the gospel reveals God's gift of justification, it does not begin there. It begins by revealing to us the wrath of God. The good news begins with this bad news: The wrath of God is pouring out of heaven upon all human sin. People defy God by ignoring him. Their sinful way of life is suppressing the truth.

I have allowed myself the freedom to range widely within the broad category "paraphrase," hovering at any given point somewhere between loose translation and sermonic exposition, depending upon the extent of explanatory enlargement judged expedient.

The prayers, on the other hand, respond to the truth lifted up in each section of Paul's letter. These prayers include affirmation of the doctrine taught, adoration of God, open receptivity to God, confession of sin, and other longings and joys appropriate in each case. My intention here is that the prayers would help you to translate the teachings of Romans into holy passions deep within your heart. Bible study without devotion, without consecration, without affections burning for God, is a travesty of true Bible study. What, after all, is the Bible for, but to lift us to God? As you read each prayer, then, think about how it responds to what Paul has been saying. Give yourself the freedom to enter into the spirit and thought of the prayer. Make it your own. That is your part in our joint project. Bring a hungry, open heart. Go hard after God. Take new steps forward in Christ, steps you have never dared to take before. Do not hold back. Nothing in your life is as important or as full of promise as your pursuit of God. Use this book to seek God more earnestly and to find him more fully.

While my paraphrase aims at representing Paul's meaning accurately, the prayers at times take liberties at the level of application. For example, in chapter 2, Paul argues that the self-righteous Jew, who cannot see himself indicted along with pagan humanity in Romans 1:18-32, is no less liable to divine wrath. My prayers, however, apply chapter 2 to Christians today. The Pharisee Paul meant to address was far from God. We believers in Christ have been brought near to God. But at times we think and behave in ways which are morally analogous to the Pharisee. My prayers assume the validity of taking this applicational step.

I have also included quotations, some of them slightly edited, which I have selected from my personal background and reading, to enlarge upon Paul's message and my prayer of response. It is impossible to anticipate which of our current expressions of faith and worship will prove to be of enduring greatness, so most of these selections are old. I realize that some readers may be unfamiliar with literary genres less commonly used today. If that is the case with you, then you are in for a treat. You will find richness and depth here. Indeed, the very antiquity of these quotations is a wholesome reminder that we are not the first generation to have discovered Jesus. The Holy Spirit has been at work in believers' hearts for a long time.

My only regret in the selection of quotations is that Patristic and Medieval writers are not more fully represented. Although I am a grateful son of the Reformation, my choices of whom to cite are not intended to exclude other branches of Christ's holy catholic church. Romans is the treasure of all who have put their faith in the Lord Jesus. And although my personal exposure to the Body of Christ is limited, my sympathies are as wide as the extent of the gospel.

You will also find section headings at the logical seams in Paul's argument, to help you track the direction of his thought.

How might you use this book most effectively? Take it in small bites, savoring the truth and allowing time for quietness before God. Toss this book into your briefcase for reading and reflection on the airplane. Or put it at your bedside for meditation at night. Or keep it at your desk for a coffee break during the day. I suggest that you read through it several times. We must be patient enough to wait for God to draw near at the time of his choosing. So read and reread. Reflect. Pray. Linger. God is not speedily summoned, as if he were our servant. But he is never far away. And if we seek him, we will find him, if we seek him with all our heart.

This could be a defining moment for you. Do not go on as you have been up to now. Determine before God to meet him anew through Romans and to get a fresh start in life. Before you begin reading through this book, do business with God. Maybe a prayer like this would make sense for you:

*O Lord, you are the God of encouragement. You are able to renew me in my faith. Let me rediscover you. Let me relearn the gospel. May this prayerful study in Romans be a new beginning for me, I pray. Speak to me, dear Lord. I open my heart to you now. In the holy name of Christ. Amen.*

If you seek God through his Word with an open, receptive heart, you *cannot* miss him. He will not *let* you miss him. He will meet you and touch you. He will rekindle your spiritual fire through the power of the gospel.

God be with you as you read, pray and ponder. May our Lord use this book to make himself more real and precious to you than he has ever been before. My joy would be boundless if this book were instrumental in renewing your life with God.

Raymond C. Ortlund, Jr.
Trinity Evangelical Divinity School
St. Barnabas' Day, 1993

# OUTLINE OF
# ROMANS

I. An Introduction to the Gospel (Romans 1:1-15)

II. A Summary of the Gospel (Romans 1:16-17)

III. An Explanation of the Gospel (Romans 1:18-5:21)

    A. The problem addressed by the gospel is this: God has consigned the entire human race, including even upright people, to domination under sin (Romans 1:18-3:20).

    B. God's answer to our problem is the cross of Christ, the benefits of which we receive by faith (Romans 3:21-5:21).

IV. The Clarification of the Gospel (Romans 6:1-11:36)

    A. By promising a surplus of grace for sinners, does the gospel throw open the door to more and more sinning, so that grace may shine all the more brightly? No, because grace unites us with Christ in his death, burial and resurrection (Romans 6:1-14).

    B. But if the gospel of abundant grace does not encourage sinning, does it still allow a casual attitude toward sin? No, because the gospel affirms that slavery to sin breeds death, while slavery to righteousness nurtures life (Romans 6:215-23).

C. Moreover, the threat of the law's condemnation does not deter sin. It only bonds us more firmly to our sin (Romans 7:1-6).

D. But if the law stirs up my sinfulness, then is the law to blame for my condition? No. My problem is my own sinful nature, which the law exposes to plain view (Romans 7:7-25).

E. But why will faith succeed where law has failed? Because the life of faith is a life in the Spirit. By his Spirit, God will make us like Christ so that we truly obey his law, and nothing can defeat his loving purpose (Romans 8:1-39).

F. But can we really trust God never to abandon us, since it appears that he has abandoned his ancient people Israel? Can we count on God's promises to be utterly sure? Yes, when we consider the ways of God (Romans 9:1-11:36).

V. The Application of the Gospel (Romans 12:1-15:13)

A. The only response to the gospel consistent with the gospel itself is to yield oneself fully to God and grow into a new life of holiness (Romans 12:1-2).

B. The gospel calls us to fit humbly and actively into the church, wherever each of us belongs (Romans 12:3-8).

C. The gospel calls us to pursue the virtues of love, both for our fellow Christians and for those who oppose the gospel's claim upon our lives (Romans 12:9-21).

D. Our life of gospel surrender also entails a cooperative spirit toward civil government (Romans 13:1-7).

E. Love is to be the pervasive flavor of gospel living (Romans 13:8-10).

F. The gospel warns us that we have little time left to clean up our lives and become fit for Christ's return (Romans 13:11-14).

G. The life of gospel surrender calls us to accept other believers when they differ from us in mattters of personal opinion (Romans 14:1-12).

H. The life of gospel surrender calls us to enjoy our freedom heedless of its effect upon other believers (Romans 14:13-23).

I. The life of gospel surrender moderates the demands of self, so that the church can, with united voice, glorify God (Romans 15:1-6).

J. Unity of heart with all true Christians is mandatory as a necessary implication of the gospel itself (Romans 15:7-13).

VI. The Fellowship of the Gospel (Romans 15:14-16:27)

A. Paul explains to the Roman church the pioneering ministry to which God has called him (Romans 15:14-21).

B. Paul enlists the Roman church's support and prayers for his ministry (Romans 15:22-33).

C. Paul introduces Phoebe, who will carry his letter to Rome, and greet his friends in the church there (Romans 16:1-16).

D. Paul adds a brief warning against false teachers (Romans 16:17-20).

E. Paul concludes with final greeting and a benediction (Romans 16:21-27).

# ROMANS
## CHAPTER 1

AN INTRODUCTION TO THE GOSPEL—ROMANS 1:1-15

**Greetings from Paul, a slave of Christ Jesus, summoned by God to serve as an apostle, set apart to a life of advancing the gospel of God.—Romans 1:1**

**PRAYER**   O sovereign Lord, I do not determine the course my life takes. You do. You have included me in your great plan for the world, at this time and in this place. I bow to your purpose for me. Deepen my sense that, in the gospel, I have something to live up to, a great purpose to be inspired by, something larger than myself to which I am duty-bound and from which I may derive direction and energy for living. And when I come to the end, O Lord, may I be found faithful. In the holy name of Christ. Amen.

> *A charge to keep I have,*
> *A God to glorify,*
> *A never-dying soul to save,*
> *And fit it for the sky.*

To *serve the present age,*
  *My calling to fulfill;*
*O may it all my powers engage,*
  *To do my Master's will!*

*Arm me with jealous care,*
  *As in thy sight to live;*
*And O, thy servant, Lord, prepare*
  *A strict account to give.*

*Help me to watch and pray,*
  *And on thyself rely,*
*And let me ne'er my trust betray,*
  *But press to realms on high.*

*Charles Wesley, 1707–1788*

❖ ❖ ❖

**This gospel God promised long ago through his prophets
in the holy writings of the Old Testament.—Romans 1:2**

**PRAYER**     O dear Lord, I love your gospel. It opens a window
into the prison of this world, letting in a shaft of heavenly light. I
look up. The light falls upon my face. It fills me with hope and joy.
   Your gospel is old. You have given me something real and
solid in the midst of my paper-thin, anti-historical pop culture.
You have given me roots that go down deeper than last week's
#1 hit. Your gospel was here long before I was, and it will endure
long after I am gone. Your ancient and holy gospel is something
for me to submit to, not to play with. Against the bias of this
present evil age which emboldens my subjectivity, quicken
within me, O Lord, a vivid sense of the antiquity and objectiv-
ity of Truth, to which my conscience must surrender, or go
deservingly to hell. In the holy name of Christ. Amen.

*One word of truth outweighs the whole world.*

> *Alexander Solzhenitsyn, 1970*

❖   ❖   ❖

This gospel is all about God's Son, who, in his humanity, descended from King David. But by his resurrection
from the dead, he was distinguished as the powerful,
Holy Spirit-anointed Son of God, Jesus Christ our Lord.
—Romans 1:3-4

**PRAYER**    You, O Lord Christ, are the great theme of the
gospel. You are King. You are Messiah. You burst forth from the
grave to receive the name that is above every name. You ascended
to glorious sovereignty at the Father's right hand. You rule and
reign from heaven, omnipotent to save. And that puts you, living Christ, at the center of the gospel message. O Lord Jesus
Christ, I own you as my Sovereign. I lay my life at your feet. Be
exalted in my life, be exalted in my heart right now, and bring
me by your merits into your everlasting kingdom, where I yearn
to be. In your holy name. Amen.

> *Thou art the King of Glory, O Christ.*
> *Thou art the everlasting Son of the Father.*
> *When thou tookest upon thee to deliver man,*
>    *thou didst not abhor the virgin's womb.*
> *When thou hadst overcome the sharpness of death,*
>    *thou didst open the Kingdom of Heaven to*
>    *all believers.*
> *Thou sittest at the right hand of God, in the glory*
>    *of the Father.*
> *We believe that thou shalt come to be our Judge.*
> *We therefore pray thee, help thy servants, whom*
>    *thou hast redeemed with thy precious blood.*

*Make them to be numbered with thy saints,*
*in glory everlasting.*

*from the* Te Deum Laudamus, *fifth century*

✧ ✧ ✧

This mighty Savior authorized me with the privilege
of apostleship, so that he would be glorified as I lay
at his feet the believing submission of the Gentiles.
You too are among this great company of believers
whom Jesus Christ has called out to be his own.
—Romans 1:5-6

PRAYER     Risen Savior, fulfill the mission of your church.
Speed the gospel into new territory, geographically and socio-
logically, through us, your servants. We long to lay at your feet
the gift of the obedience of the nations. Deliver us from cultural
relativism, which trivializes your gospel as the religion of one particular human tradition only and discourages bold missionary
enterprise. Give us clarity of doctrinal vision and courage of
moral conviction to march forward through the opposition to
solid accomplishment, for your gospel is the truth. And, O Lord,
as you move by your Spirit from nation to nation, from city to
city, from church to church, do not pass me by. O dear Lord,
draw near! In your holy name. Amen.

*Listen! Hear the Lord of harvest calling: Who will go*
*and work for me today? Who will bring to me the*
*lost and dying? Who will point them to the narrow*
*way? Speak, my Lord. Speak, and I'll be quick to*
*answer thee. Speak, and I will answer, "Here am I,*
*send me."*

*Harold J. Ockenga, 1958*

✧ ✧ ✧

To the whole Church in Rome, loved by God, called to be holy. Grace and peace to you from God our Father and our Lord Jesus Christ.—Romans 1:7

**PRAYER**    You come to us, Father, greeting us with the kiss of grace and peace. We love you now, only because you loved us first. Your love is not general and sentimental and indulgent. It is individually directed and morally purposeful. Your love calls us to be holy, even as you are holy. And you have lavished upon us all the graces and victories we so urgently need, in our weakness, for your sacred calling to be fulfilled in us. Enlarge our hearts with true love for you, O God, and quicken our resolve to show it with true holiness of life. In the name of Christ. Amen.

> *O mercy, from what abundant sweetness and sweet abundance do you flow forth to us! O measureless goodness of God, with what affection must you be loved by sinners! O measureless goodness, passing all understanding, let that mercy which proceeds from your great wealth come upon me! It flows forth from you; let it flow into me!*
>
> *Anselm, ca. 1033–1109*

✧ ✧ ✧

To begin, I want you to know that I offer my God thanks, through Jesus Christ, for you all. Your faith is being spoken of everywhere. God knows that with deep yearnings of soul I serve the cause of the gospel of his Son by offering constant prayers for you. I am continually asking God that, as soon as he wills, I may at last be sped on my way to you.—Romans 1:8-10

**PRAYER**    O Lord, visit your church today with authentic faith, a conspicuous and influential faith. Make us famous, not primarily for having big organizations but for demonstrating a big faith. Make us into a church that is *worth* talking about. O God, for your glory's sake, empower your church with a convincing witness today. And for myself, dear Lord, let me be faithful in the work of intercession, unknown to the public eye but so vital in all true ministry. Let me never lose my quietness before you. Let me never become weary in prayer. Keep alive in my weak heart a jealous love for your church and for your cause, a confident expectation of answers to my prayers, as I plead that your kingdom advance in the world through the renewal of your church today. In the holy name of Christ. Amen.

> *God speaks of himself as standing ready to be gracious to his church and to appear for its restoration, and only waiting for such an opportunity to bestow this mercy when he shall hear the cries of his people for it, that he may bestow it in answer to their prayers. Isaiah 30:18-19: "Therefore will the Lord wait, that he may be gracious to thee; . . . he will be very gracious unto thee at the voice of thy cry; when he shall hear it, he will answer thee." The words imply that when God once sees his people much engaged in praying for this mercy, it shall be no longer delayed.*
>
> *Jonathan Edwards, 1703–1758*

❖  ❖  ❖

For I long to come visit you, so that I may strengthen you with some gift of spiritual benefit, as your needs may require. I mean, of course, a *mutual* exchange of blessing, since you will contribute to my faith as well. Please do not get the wrong impression, dear friends. My absence from

Rome is not due to indifference toward you. I have often planned to come—so far, every attempt frustrated!—so that I may reap a spiritual harvest among you, just as I aim to do among all the Gentiles. I have a responsibility to bring the gospel to everyone everywhere, both to the civilized and to the uncivilized, to the sophisticated and to the simple. It is this sense of responsibility, not mere ambition, that explains my urgency to come minister the gospel to you in Rome.—Romans 1:11-15

**PRAYER**     O Lord, how trivial are my aspirations and desires. I pursue the amusements and toys and carnality of the modern world, while the higher longings of my soul weaken from neglect. What do I need to *remove* from my life, in order to throw myself without reserve or impediment into the great cause of the gospel? This is my brief moment in history. I do not have forever. Now is my time to speak to my generation. Purify my heart, Lord. Energize my desires. Open my eyes. Compel me with my personal responsibility to serve the interests of the gospel in the world today. O Lord, let me spend my life for you, disregarding all risks, accepting all consequences. Let the power of the gospel so grip me that I act upon it, come what may. Let me recover the power to live and to die for my faith. In the holy name of Christ. Amen.

> *To eat, to breathe*
> *to beget*
> *Is this all there is*
> *Chance configuration of atom against atom*
>     *of god against god*
> *I cannot believe it.*
> *Come, Christian Triune God who lives,*
> *Here am I*
> *Shake the world again.*
>
>                     *Francis Schaeffer, 1960*

✧   ✧   ✧

## A SUMMARY OF THE GOSPEL—ROMANS 1:16-17

Wherever I go with the gospel, I go with confidence and joy, because the gospel works with the power of Almighty God to save people—anyone and everyone who believes—including the Jew first, of course, but also the Gentile. In particular, the gospel reveals God's way of restoring sinners to his favor, and his way of justification is marked throughout, from first to last, by the principle of faith. As it is written, "The one who is justified *by faith* will enter into true life."—Romans 1:16-17

**PRAYER**    O God, what a treasure I have in your gospel! You show me there what no therapist can do, what no government program can do, what no money can buy. Your gospel shows how you give a sinner like me a fresh start in life and a glorious destiny in eternity. And I don't have to trigger this wonderful change with my own power or virtue. I receive it with the empty hands of faith. O Lord, I do now receive the full merit of my Savior to wash away all my guilt forever and to procure for me everlasting joy in your presence above. I receive the continual flow of his meritorious obedience washing over me, covering all my sins, compensating for all my guilt and fulfilling all my failed obligations to you, placing me in your presence as one fully measuring up to the standards of your holy law. Fill me now with deeper, richer affections for you, prompted by the blessed Holy Spirit, as you enlarge my understanding of your gospel. In the holy name of Christ. Amen.

*Justification by faith is an answer to the greatest personal question ever asked by a human soul: "How shall I be right with God? How do I stand in God's sight?*

*With what favor does he look upon me?" There are those, I admit, who never raise that question. There are those who are concerned with the question of their standing before men but never with the question of their standing before God. There are those who are interested in what "people say" but not in the question what God says. Such men, however, are not those who move the world. They are apt to go with the current. They are apt to do as others do. They are not the heroes who change the destinies of the race. The beginning of true nobility comes when a man ceases to be interested in the judgment of men and becomes interested in the judgment of God.*

*J. Gresham Machen, 1881–1937*

*I greatly longed to understand Paul's Epistle to the Romans, and nothing stood in the way but that one expression, "the righteousness of God," because I took it to mean that righteousness whereby God is righteous and deals righteously in punishing the unrighteous. My situation was that, although an impeccable monk, I stood before God as a sinner troubled in conscience, and I had no confidence that my merit would assuage him. Therefore I did not love a righteous and angry God but rather hated and murmured against him. Yet I clung to the dear Paul and had a great yearning to know what he meant. Night and day I pondered until I saw the connection between the righteousness of God and the statement that "the righteous one shall live by his faith." Then I grasped that the righteousness of God is that righteousness by which, through grace and sheer mercy, God justifies us by faith. Thereupon I felt myself to be reborn and to have gone through open doors into paradise. The whole of Scripture took on a*

*new meaning, and whereas before "the righteousness*
*of God" had filled me with hate, now it became to me*
*inexpressibly sweet in greater love. This passage of*
*Paul became to me a gateway to heaven.*

*Martin Luther, 1483–1546*

❖ ❖ ❖

## AN EXPLANATION OF THE GOSPEL—ROMANS 1:18-5:21

THE PROBLEM ADDRESSED by the gospel is this: God has consigned the entire human race, including even upright people, to domination under sin—Romans 1:18-3:20

THE WRATH OF GOD is pouring out on sinful mankind
—Romans 1:18-32

> While the gospel reveals God's gift of justification, it does not begin there. It begins by revealing to us the wrath of God. The good news begins with this bad news: The wrath of God is pouring out of heaven upon all human sin. People defy God by ignoring him. Their sinful way of life is suppressing the truth.—Romans 1:18

PRAYER    O God, you are just. Your wrath is just. There is something deep down inside us all that wants to rub you out of existence, so that we can live as our own gods. We treat you as if you were unreal and try to construct an alternative reality through alternative lifestyles. And the root of it all is a radical defiance against your authority over us. O God, your wrath is just.

But, dear Lord, you are also merciful. You are merciful even to alert us to your wrath, so that we may bow before you and receive your pardon. I do bow to you right now. I affirm that you are real. I affirm your rightful ultimacy over me. Let my life be a demonstration, not a denial, of your reality, O God. In the holy name of Christ. Amen.

> *I was sitting in our apartment on St. Paul Street in Baltimore. . . . My daughter was in her high chair. I was watching her eat. She was the most miraculous thing that had ever happened in my life. I liked to watch her even when she smeared porridge on her face or dropped it meditatively on the floor. My eye came to rest on the delicate convolutions of her ear—those intricate, perfect ears. The thought passed through my mind: "No, those ears were not created by any chance coming together of atoms in nature. . . . They could have been created only by immense design." The thought was involuntary and unwanted. I crowded it out of my mind. . . . I had to crowd it out of my mind. If I had completed it, I should have had to say: Design presupposes God.*

> *Whittaker Chambers, 1952*
> *recalling his former life as an atheist*

❖  ❖  ❖

And the reason why this draws from God a response of wrath is that the truth is so obvious to everyone. God made it to be obvious. And the obvious truth is that God is there, in all his eternal power and deity. Anyone can see that from the creation, looking around thoughtfully. So if we do not know God, it can only be that we do not *want* to know God, and that kind of ignorance is damnable.—Romans 1:19-20

**PRAYER**    O God, you are God. The fact that you are invisible gives us no excuse for not knowing you. We are surrounded by clearly revealed evidences of your presence and power. We *are* such evidences ourselves. Even when we defy you, our very capacity to do so bespeaks your existence. So disregarding you, marginalizing you, denying you, must be ignorance-by-choice. O Creator, how does my life contradict the truth of your eternal power and deity? Where am I protecting a convenient lie? Plant the flag of your kingdom at that very place in my soul. Turn my defeats into your triumphs, so that I *want* to know you, so that I *want* to walk through life acknowledging you and enjoying you in all things. In the holy name of Christ. Amen.

*From harmony, from heav'nly harmony*
*This universal frame began.*
*When nature underneath a heap*
*Of jarring atoms lay,*
*And could not heave her head,*
*The tuneful Voice was heard from high,*
*"Arise, ye more than dead."*
*Then cold and hot and moist and dry*
*In order to their stations leap,*
*And Music's pow'r obey.*
*From harmony, from heav'nly harmony*
*This universal frame began.*
*From harmony to harmony,*
*Through all the compass of the notes it ran,*
*The diapason closing full in Man.*

*John Dryden, 1687*
*"A Song for St. Cecilia's Day"*

*We know God by two means: first, by the creation, preservation and government of the universe, which is before our eyes like a most elegant book, wherein all creatures, great and small, are as so many characters leading us to contemplate the invisible things of God, namely, his eternal power and Godhead, as the Apostle Paul says. All which things are sufficient to convince men and leave them without excuse. Second, he makes*

*himself more clearly and fully known to us by his holy*
*and divine Word, that is to say, as far as is necessary for*
*us to know in this life, for his glory and our salvation.*

*The Belgic Confession, 1561*

✧ ✧ ✧

The world's ignorance of God is no accident. They knew
him once, but they refused to give him the glory and
thanks that, as God, he deserves. And so they have lost
touch with reality. Their reasoning is nonsense. Their
irrational minds are darkened. Boasting superior wisdom, expert knowledge and advanced degrees, their con-
clusions are stupid. Look at the record of human religion.
People have exchanged the worship of the immortal God
in all his glory, for what? Now they bow down before
images of mortal man—even worse, of birds, of animals
and, as if there were no depth to which they will not
stoop, even of snakes!—Romans 1:21-23

**PRAYER** O God, never let me trivialize you. Never let me mis-
represent you. Let me know you aright and worship you in all
your true glory. Dispel the darkness of my natural religious
instincts and flood my mind with a true vision of your majesty, as
I subordinate my thinking to Holy Scripture. O God, let me know
you in truth, as you really are. In the holy name of Christ. Amen.

*What are you, O Lord, what are you? How shall my heart*
*think of you? Certainly you are life, you are wisdom, you*
*are truth, you are goodness, you are blessedness, you are*
*eternity, and you are every true good. But these are many,*
*and my narrow understanding cannot take in so much in a*
*single glance and take delight in all at once.*

*Anselm, ca. 1033–1109*

✧ ✧ ✧

This is why God has handed the human race over to the power of their sin. Left to themselves, they are now at the mercy of unrestrained desire. The result is that, with their filthy pleasures, they have degraded themselves and one another in the prison of sensuality. This is what they get for exchanging the truth of who God really is for the lie that they can be their own gods. They reverence and serve what is created rather than the Creator—who, in actual fact, is the forever blessed fountain of all true life. Amen.—Romans 1:24-25

**PRAYER**    O God, what a horrific thing it is to live without you. What a hellish thing it is to live at the mercy of desire. How degrading to be reduced to an animal-like existence, devoid of the things of the Spirit. And I thought that I would be like God! I thought that I would take control! Your law of unintended consequences works with infallible inevitability. But this is just, because it is not true that I am God. You alone are God. You alone deserve my reverence. You are, even at this moment, worshiped in heaven by beings superior to me. How can I be so evil, so stupid, so dull, as to challenge you? I judge myself a wicked fool, and I worship you as the eternally blessed God, the source of life in its fullness. Lord above, I do adore you now as my only true joy. In the holy name of Christ. Amen.

*Whatever your heart is most set upon, that is your God. Therefore, you must know that this is the meaning of the commandment, "Thou shalt have no other Gods before me." That is, you shall give Me, and nothing else, the strength of your soul. I am a God to My creature when I have its strength exercised about Me, to lift up Me as the highest good. But if there is any-*

*thing else that your soul is set on as the highest good,*
*that's your god, and it's worse than bowing the knee.*
*You bow your soul to that thing.*

Jeremiah Burroughs, 1599–1646

❖ ❖ ❖

This is why God has released the human race to domination by their own impulses. Ruled now by passion rather than principle, they fall into shameful lusts for one another. They are so gripped by the irrational power of sin that their natural desires are twisted into unnatural. Women have sex with women. And men turn away from natural sexual relations with women and burn with lust for one another. Men with men, they do obscene things with each other, getting back for it the inevitable consequence—more of their own perversion.—Romans 1:26-27

**PRAYER** O Lord, is there anything so low, so base, so disgusting, that our natural morality will refuse to condone it? Your gospel teaches me that there is not. Our corruption is so profound that we are prepared, if sufficiently motivated, to violate any and every boundary of nature, taste and common sense. But I can see why. If we deny that you are God and we are not God, what will keep us from denying that a man is a man and not a woman? When we deny you, any denial of obvious truth becomes thinkable.

But, Lord, even we who have never fallen into these particular sins of passion can see in them the same *principle* of perversity that all human nature, ourselves included, shares together in a universal fallenness. O God, we will never lift ourselves up out of what we are. How can we, when we ourselves are sinful in our very natures? We need a new nature within. Write your holy law on this perverse heart of mine, dear Lord. In the holy name of Christ. Amen.

*It is indeed common for men to conceal their faults
and gratify their passions in secret and especially,
when they are first initiated in vice, to make use
rather of artifice and dissimulation than audacious-
ness and effrontery. But the arts of hypocrisy are in
time exhausted and some unhappy circumstance
defeats those measures which they had laid for pre-
venting a discovery. They are at length suspected, and
by that curiosity which suspicion always excites,
closely pursued and openly detected. It is then too
late to think of deceiving mankind by false appearances, nor does anything remain but to avow boldly
what can no longer be denied. Impudence is called in
to the assistance of immorality, and the censures,
which cannot be escaped, must be openly defied.
Wickedness is in itself timorous and naturally skulks
in coverts and in darkness, but grows furious by
despair and, when it can fly no farther, turns upon the
pursuer. Such is the state of a man abandoned to the
indulgence of vicious inclinations. He justifies one
crime with another, invents wicked principles to support wicked practices, endeavors rather to corrupt
others than own himself corrupted and to avoid that
shame which a confession of his crimes would bring
upon him, calls evil good and good evil, puts darkness
for light and light for darkness. . . . Wickedness in this
state seems to have extended its power from the passions to the understanding. Not only the desire of
doing well is extinguished, but the discernment of
good and evil is obliterated and destroyed. Such is the
infatuation produced by a long course of obstinate
guilt. Not only our speculations influence our practice, but our practice reciprocally influences our speculations. We not only do what we approve, but there
is danger lest in time we come to approve what we
do, though for no other reason but that we do it. A*

*man is always desirous of being at peace with himself,*
*and when he cannot reconcile his passions to his con-*
*science, he will attempt to reconcile his conscience to*
*his passions.*

*Samuel Johnson, 1709–1784*

✧  ✧  ✧

This is why God has let the human race go. They have
not considered God worth knowing, so God has abandoned them to worthlessness. He has dulled their moral
intuitions, so that they violate conscience and right. They
are brimming with all sorts of wrong, malice, greed,
spite. They are full of envy, murder, conflict, treachery,
putting everything in the worst light. They are whisper-
ers, backbiters, bitter toward God, insolent, arrogant,
boastful, fascinated with evil, disobedient to parents,
unwise, untrue, unloving, unmerciful. And in spite of the
warnings of conscience, alerting them that God judges
such lives with death, they not only go ahead and sin anyway but they also cheer others on in the same evil
course.—Romans 1:28-32

**PRAYER**    O God, I am no different. My life is consistent
with this larger, damning account of human sinfulness. I confess and bewail that I have added my own personal contribution to this record of wickedness. The fact is, Lord, I cannot
help myself. Sin is running in my veins. Rinse it out of me, O
Savior God, or I will die! The one thing I *must* have—your
favor upon me—is the very thing I *cannot* have, because you
are holy and I am sinful. A death sentence hangs over me, unless
you save me from the guilt and power of my sins. O Lord, what
will your gospel teach me of that? I yearn to know it. In the holy
name of Christ. Amen.

*Is it to be thought a small misery, not to love you? Woe
is me! Tell me for your mercy's sake, O Lord my God,
what you are to me. Say to my soul, "I am your salvation!" Speak it out, that I may hear you. Behold, the ears
of my heart are before you, O Lord. Open them and say
unto my soul, "I am your salvation!" I will run after
that voice and take hold of you. Hide not your face from
me. Let me die, lest I die, that I may see your face.*

*Augustine, 354–430*

# ROMANS

## CHAPTER 2

MORALLY UPRIGHT PEOPLE are equally as guilty before God
—Romans 2:1-11

> And as for you, Mr. Moral High Ground, you too are
> without excuse! You cannot point an accusing finger at
> that pagan world out there without condemning yourself
> as well. You are no different. Your very inclination to
> write off the rest of humanity as morally inferior exposes
> your own hypocrisy, because you do the very same
> things.—Romans 2:1

PRAYER    O God, I, a Bible-believing, church-going Christian,
am thoroughly worldly. My faith is culture-bound and morally
compromised. My impulses leap toward the same things the
world idolizes—ego, money, recognition, power, ease, privilege.
How partial, how conveniently self-serving, are my grand moral
indictments of others. O God, your judgment is just. In the holy
name of Christ. Amen.

*I cannot pray, but I sin. I cannot hear or preach a sermon, but I sin. I cannot give an alms or receive the sacrament, but I sin. Nay, I cannot so much as confess my sins, but my confessions are still aggravations of them. My repentance needs to be repented of, my tears want washing, and the very washing of my tears needs still to be washed over again with the blood of my Redeemer.*

*William Beveridge, 1638–1708*

❖   ❖   ❖

We all grant that God's judgment of sinful mankind is morally valid. Now do you really think that, doing the very things yourself that you condemn in others, *you* will be exempted from God's judgment? Or would you cheapen the abundance of his kindness? Is it worth anything to you that God has thus far delayed judgment? Do you spurn God's patience with you? Don't you realize that his kindness is intended to draw out of you the very opposite response, namely, repentance? —Romans 2:2-4

**PRAYER**    O God, we mistake your patient withholding of judgment for a weak indifference toward judgment. But, in truth, your mighty judgment passes no one by, not even me. And you have put up with so much from me for so long. Time and again, you have given me another chance when you could have snuffed me out. Let me take full advantage of this present moment of grace by telling you I am sorry for my sins. Let me walk before you in a spirit of humble gratitude. Let my frozen heart be melted by your mercies. And let your longsuffering kindness toward me be matched by ready repentance from me. O God, give me the treasure of a broken and contrite heart, before it is too late. I do not have forever. In the holy name of Christ. Amen.

> *There is a holy sacrifice*
> *Which God in heaven will not despise,*
> *Yes, which is precious in his eyes,*
> *The contrite heart.*

> *That lofty One, before whose throne*
> *The countless hosts of heaven bow down,*
> *Another dwelling place will own,*
> *The contrite heart.*

> *The Holy One, the Son of God,*
> *His pardoning love will shed abroad,*
> *And consecrate as his abode,*
> *The contrite heart.*

> *The Holy Spirit from on high*
> *Will listen to its faintest cry,*
> *And cheer and bless and purify*
> *The contrite heart.*

> *Savior, I cast my hopes on thee;*
> *Such as thou art, I too would be;*
> *In mercy, Lord, bestow on me*
> *The contrite heart.*

> *Charlotte Elliott, 1789–1871*

✧ ✧ ✧

But, as it is, your unresponsive, self-righteous heart is winning for you God's wrath on that final day of wrath, when God will reveal with solemn finality his righteous judgment.—Romans 2:5

**PRAYER**    O God, you have given me warning. You have clearly declared that you will reveal your wrath against sin with unalterably eternal judgment on that day. Give me eyes to see this brief *now* in connection with that awful *then*. Nurture within me a true fear of you, to prepare me for that day. In the holy name of Christ. Amen.

> *Lord, in this thy mercy's day,*
> *Ere it wholly pass away,*
> *On our knees we fall and pray.*
>
> *Holy Jesus, grant us tears,*
> *Fill us with heart-searching fears,*
> *Ere that awful doom appears.*
>
> *Lord, on us thy Spirit pour,*
> *Kneeling lowly at thy door,*
> *Ere it close forevermore.*
>
> *Judge and Savior of our race,*
> *When we see thee face to face,*
> *Grant us 'neath thy wings a place.*
>
> *Isaac Williams, 1802–1865*

✧   ✧   ✧

God will deal out to each one a judgment that matches the way he has lived his life. To those who, by steadfastly persevering in godliness, seek glory, honor and immortality, God will grant the richness and fullness of life forever. But to those whose lives are marked by unprincipled ambition, skepticism toward the truth and cynical reliance on the devices of wickedness, he will pour out wrath and fury. He will impose distress and anguish upon every human being whose life shows a pattern of evil, to the Jew first and also to the Gentile. But he will give glory and honor and peace to every one whose life reveals true virtue, to the Jew first and also to the Gentile. For God applies the same standard of judgment to all alike.—Romans 2:6-11

**PRAYER**   O God, how clear your moral vision is, compared with mine. Looking out upon the world, I see an infinite number of moral classes. Looking out over the same world, you perceive only two—the good and the evil. And you judge all mankind by that simple but profound standard. How searching is your gaze! How deeply it penetrates, seeing through appearances into reality! What do you see in me? O God, have mercy. Let me live today in such a way that I may have no regrets when I come to tomorrow. Let me lay a firm foundation for eternity, by your grace and mercy. In the holy name of Christ. Amen.

> *As the tree falls,*
> *So must it lie;*
> *As the man lives,*
> *So will he die;*
> *As the man dies,*
> *Such must he be*
> *All through the days*
> *Of eternity.*
>
> *Edward Caswall, 1814-1878*

✧  ✧  ✧

NOT JUST *knowing* what is right, but only *doing* what is right, matters to God—Romans 2:12-16

While all who have sinned in ignorance of God's law will perish for reasons other than that law, all who have

sinned in conscious defiance of his law will be condemned by the law. Why? Because no one with a merely theoretical knowledge of the righteousness God's law requires will be justified before God. Only those with actual, demonstrated righteousness will be justified.
—Romans 2:12-13

**PRAYER**    O God, possessing a true knowledge of your moral standards can make me feel so virtuous. I look out over the pagan masses with smug self-righteousness and tell myself, "Well, at least I *know* the difference between right and wrong, which is more than can be said of *them*!" How deceitful my sin is. How empty my virtue is. O God, deliver me from big-talking hypocrisy and impart to me a true faith, a real faith, that is more eager to bear fruit in practical godliness than to condemn others. In the holy name of Christ. Amen.

*If contempt for the temporal and concern for the eternal are necessary attitudes for Christians, it is necessary that these attitudes appear in the whole course of their lives. If self-denial be a condition for salvation, all who would be saved must make self-denial a part of their everyday life. If humility be a Christian duty, then the everyday life of a Christian is to be a constant course of humility. If we are to relieve the naked, the sick, and the prisoner, such expression of love must be the constant effort of our lives. If we are to love our enemies, we must make our common life a visible exercise and demonstration of that love. If contentment and thankfulness be duties to God, they are the duties of every day and in every circumstance of our lives. If we are to be wise and holy as the newborn sons of God, we must renounce everything that is foolish and vain in every part of our daily life. If we*

*are to be new creatures in Christ, we must show that*
*we are so by new ways of living in the world. If we*
*are to follow Christ, it must be in the way we spend*
*each day.*

William Law, 1686–1761

❖ ❖ ❖

When Gentiles obey God out of their natural moral
instincts rather than in conscious obedience to the law of
Moses, they are acknowledging that such a thing as
moral law exists, even though they do not know God's
*revealed* moral law. They are giving evidence that a
sense of right and wrong is deeply imprinted on their
hearts. Their consciences testify to this God-given moral
sensibility with thoughts of self-accusation and even self-
approval. But God will clear away all moral ambiguity
on that day when, through Jesus Christ, he will judge
these secrets of our hearts, as my gospel teaches he
will.—Romans 2:14-16

**PRAYER**   O God, by a misplaced sense of mercy I might
wish to exempt from your judgment those who have never
heard your truth. But they do have *a* word, if not *the* Word,
from you, for they have the voice of conscience—which no
one consistently obeys. O Lord, how prone I am to a sentimental gospel. But your truth preserves the moral dignity and
solemn responsibility of every human being, without exception. O Father, let me not deny or evade the light *I* possess.
Quicken my heart to be as responsive as it is enlightened. Let
your light shine into my darkness, and do not let my darkness
overcome it.

   O Christ, you are not only the Savior of the world, you are
also our Judge. And you will not judge the human race super-

ficially, as our fallible judges do. You will sift through our most
secret thoughts, for all is laid bare before you. We are not fool-
ing you for a moment. You know us. You see through us. You
search us with eyes like a flame of fire. O holy Christ, there is
refuge in you now, but there will be no refuge from you then.
All-seeing Judge, I flee to you for mercy now. In your holy
name. Amen.

> *That day of wrath, that dreadful day,*
> *When heaven and earth shall pass away,*
> *What power shall be the sinner's stay?*
> *How shall he meet that dreadful day?*
>
> *When, shrivelling like a parchèd scroll,*
> *The flaming heavens together roll,*
> *When, louder yet, and yet more dread,*
> *Swells the high trump that wakes the dead,*
>
> *O, on that day, that wrathful day,*
> *When man to judgment wakes from clay,*
> *Be thou the trembling sinner's stay,*
> *Though heaven and earth shall pass away!*
>
> Sir Walter Scott, 1771–1832

❖　❖　❖

OUTWARD IDENTIFICATION WITH the covenant guarantees nothing, if you disobey its moral entailments—Romans 2:17-24

But if you bear the noble identity of Jew, one set apart
to God by covenant, then let's take your own case. You
rest your hopes on your scrupulous observance of the
law and flatter yourself on your special relationship with
God. You know what he wants from you and can dis-

tinguish the weightier matters of the law, having been well schooled in it. You are confident that you qualify as a guide to the spiritually blind, that you shine like a light in the midst of the surrounding moral darkness. You can correct the ignorant and teach spiritual babes, for you possess in the law God's definitive statement of spiritual knowledge and absolute truth. Now, Mr. Moral High Ground, don't you teach *yourself*? You are the one preaching against stealing. Do *you* steal? You are the one warning others not to commit adultery. Do *you* commit adultery? You are the one who loathes idols. Do *you* desecrate that which is holy? You feel so superior, because you know God's law. But you dishonor God by violating that very law. Your life is exactly what the Scripture talks about when it says, "The name of God is desecrated among the Gentiles because of your hypocrisy!"—Romans 2:17-24

**PRAYER** O God in heaven, we, your church, see ourselves today as the salt of the earth and the light of the world. And so we are. Or are we? Do we live up to this high and holy calling? Our sexual scandals, our financial crookedness, our doctrinal superficiality, our televised foolishness, our cynical competition between Christian organizations, our addiction to fads, our secularized methods, our hypocrisies, heresies and absurdities—and we wonder why we aren't more influential for good! Our moral influence is weak, because our moral character is weak. The world doesn't take you seriously, because we ourselves have given them ample reason not to. O God, we are too ashamed to lift our eyes to heaven. But we are still your blood-bought church. You purchased us at a high cost and lovingly bound us to yourself through the eternal covenant. O Christ, we cling to your merit as our only warrant for confidence. O Spirit, we yearn for you to renew us and reform us. O Triune God, make your church majestic in the world today, to your own greater glory. Oh that you would rend the heavens and come down, that the mountains of sin in the church and in the world might quake at your presence, that the nations might tremble at your presence! In the holy name of Christ. Amen.

*Christians, ye who profess to desire a revival of religion and to make this a commanding subject of your prayers, let me ask whether . . . you have no reason to fear that you may yourselves be standing in the way of the bestowment of the very blessing for which you profess to plead. The great obstacles to the revival of God's work are no doubt to be sought in the church. . . . And I appeal to each of your consciences, as in the presence of the Searcher of the heart, whether the guilt of hindering God's work . . . does not lie at your door. Why is it that the Holy Spirit is not now as manifestly in the midst of us by his awakening and converting influences as he has been in other days? Is it not because you have relapsed in some measure into a habit of worldliness? Or because you value the blessing less? Or because you are less united and vigorous in your efforts to obtain it? Christians, awake, one and all, to a deeper sense of your responsibility. Let it not be told in heaven that God's people on earth are posing obstacles to the salvation of perishing men. In doing this, ye parents, ye may be keeping your own children out of heaven. . . . But you cannot do this and think what you are doing. It must be that you are acting incautiously. Awake then to solemn reflection. Awake to earnest prayer. Awake to faithful and persevering action.*

*William B. Sprague, 1795–1876*

✧  ✧  ✧

A NEW NATURE WITHIN, not the outward covenant sign alone, marks the true Jew—Romans 2:25-29

As a sign of the covenant, Jewish circumcision really is worth something—but only if you obey the law of the covenant. If, however, you live in heedless disregard of God's moral law, your circumcision has no meaning. Conversely, if an uncircumcised Gentile gives evidence of a real faith by obeying God's holy law, won't his uncircumcised condition be regarded as virtual circumcision, including him in the circle of covenant blessing? And that physically uncircumcised Gentile who keeps God's law will by his life condemn you, who for all your biblical credentials and circumcision still break the law. So here is my point. A Jew who is marked by the outward sign alone is not a true Jew, nor is the kind of circumcision performed as a merely outward surgical procedure true circumcision. The true Jew is marked by a new heart within. And true circumcision is a matter of inner, spiritual surgery on one's sinful self, performed by the Holy Spirit and not in merely outward compliance with the biblical regulation. This kind of hidden, personal transformation may not be esteemed by men, but it means everything to God.—Romans 2:25-29

PRAYER    O God, cut it away. Cut away this thing inside. Cut away this corrupt nature within me. Go down to the very root of my most private hypocrisies, deep within, and dig it out. Your touch, I know, will be painful. But my natural condition will kill me anyway. So open me up. Take it out. I yearn to be rid of it all. And put a new nature in its place, a heart full of unfeigned, simple goodness. Mark me deep down inside as your covenant child. But do not let me go on in my natural condition, so congenial with all that is shameful. O God, cut it away and put it to death. Let me die, that I may live. In the holy name of Christ. Amen.

Come down, O Love divine, seek thou this soul
   of mine,
And visit it with thine own ardor glowing.
   O Comforter, draw near.
   Within my heart appear,
And kindle it, thy holy flame bestowing.

O let it freely burn, 'til earthly passions turn
To dust and ashes in its heat consuming.
   And let thy glorious light
   Shine ever on my sight,
And clothe me round, the while my path illuming.

Let holy charity mine outward vesture be
And lowliness become mine inner clothing—
   True lowliness of heart,
   Which takes the humbler part
And o'er its own shortcomings weeps with loathing.

And so the yearning strong, with which the
   soul will long,
Shall far outpass the power of human telling.
   For none can guess its grace,
   'Til he become the place
Wherein the Holy Spirit makes his dwelling.

                              Bianco da Siena, ?–1434

# ROMANS

## CHAPTER 3

THE ARGUMENT OF chapter two does not negate the significance
of being Jewish, but it does magnify the faithfulness of God
—Romans 3:1-4

> Given what I have just argued, what then is the advan-
> tage of being Jewish? Or what good does covenant cir-
> cumcision do? Being Jewish is a privilege rich in many
> ways! For one thing, the Jewish nation was given the
> responsibility of receiving, treasuring and obeying all the
> revelations of God from Abraham to Jesus Christ. True,
> some Jews have responded with unbelief. But so what?
> Their lack of faith cannot defeat God's faithfulness, can
> it? Unthinkable! God will be true to his word, whatever
> breach of faith is found in man! Scripture affirms the
> infinitely superior moral character of God compared
> with the utterly discredited moral character of man when
> it says to God,
>
> *You are vindicated when you pass sentence,*
> *you triumph when you render judgment.*

—Romans 3:1-4

**PRAYER** O God, how richly you have poured out privilege upon the Christian church, just as you did upon the Jewish nation. We are especially rich with the privilege of possessing truth in your revealed Word.

O Lord, give us grace to respond with a full and uncompromised faith. Grant to your church today great meltings of heart under your Word. Do not let us think that we know better than you do, that your truth is less relevant today and must be adjusted to the times. We cannot improve upon your Word, O Lord. You are always right. You are always vindicated. You always triumph. Renew in us today a sensitive and glad submission to your Word of truth, so worthy of all acceptance. Do not let us resist you, for we cannot outsmart you. In the holy name of Christ. Amen.

*The first symptom of revival which I mention is an unusual thirst for the preaching of the Word and unusual meltings of soul under it. Observe how it is with the newborn babe. It thirsts, by the power of an irresistible instinct, after its mother's milk, the destined food and nourishment of its infant life. Just so it is with the heaven-born soul, and with the new-born revived church. It thirsts, by the force of a resistless spiritual instinct, after "the sincere milk of the Word," the food and nourishment of the immortal soul. In dead souls and dead churches, there is nothing even approaching to a thirst for the preaching of the Word. The people come to the house of God not to satisfy an appetite but to discharge a duty. The most solemn and affecting truths fall powerless on their ears. There are no meltings, no subduings of soul under them. They are scarce listened to without impatience, unless there be something remarkable and exciting in the style and manner of address. Very possibly, eloquence may moisten the eyes and touch the feelings of the people; but the most affecting truths of God fail of reaching their hearts. . . . The whole of this is reversed in a revived, a living church. The souls of the people there open at once to the Word of God, melt and bend beneath the most simple truths presented in the simplest Scripture dress. Every opportunity is eagerly embraced. New opportunities are desired and longed for. The Word is drunk in with an avidity and delight before unknown. . . . Let one example suffice from the account of the Isle of Skye: "It was a common thing, as soon as the Bible was opened, after the preliminary services, and just as the reader began"— here, you will observe, it was the simple reading of the Word without preaching—yet such was the power upon the minds of the people that "it was a common thing for great meltings to come upon the hearers. The deepest attention was paid to every word as the sacred verses were slowly and solemnly enunciated. Then the silent tear might be seen stealing down the rugged but expressive countenances turned upon the reader. It was often a stirring sight to witness the multitudes assembling during the dark winter evenings, to trace their progress as they came in all directions across moors and mountains by the blazing torches which they carried to light their way to the places of meeting. The Word of the Lord was precious in those days, and personal inconvenience was little thought of when the hungering soul sought to be satisfied."*

*Charles J. Brown, 1806–1884*

❖   ❖   ❖

BUT THE FACT that human sin has a certain usefulness in the ways of God does not excuse that sin from divine judgment—Romans 3:5-8

But if our sinfulness sets off God's triumphant righteousness all the more brilliantly, what should we con-

clude? That God is unfair to punish us with his wrath? (I apologize for stooping to the logic of our natural hypocrisy.) Such a conclusion is unthinkable! If it *were* true that our sins deserve God's indulgence because they make him look good, then what warrant would he have for judging the world? And surely, God is too just to allow human sin to go forever unanswered. But since it is true that God's truthfulness is glorified all the more by our falsehood, it has been objected, "Why then does God punish me as a sinner? Aren't my sins doing him a favor?" But by that line of reasoning one could conclude that we should sin all the more to accomplish all the more ultimate good. And some people libelously allege that I do teach this. Their damnation is just.
—Romans 3:5-8

**PRAYER**    O holy God, your wrath is neither impulsive nor neurotic nor hypocritical. It is just. It is right. It is fair. We deserve it. Our hypocrisy deserves it. We resort to any clever excuse, however preposterous, to rationalize our guilt. But our evasive tactics only prove, O God, that you are in the right. Never, never, never let me twist your truth into an excuse for allowing my evil. Rid my mind of such devilish thinking. While I humble myself before you right now, O Lord, renew my mind with exalted and reverent thoughts of your righteousness and with a loathing hatred for my own sinfulness. In the holy name of Christ. Amen.

*Dear brethren, I pray you in God's name to think of this. If punishment comes from the righteousness of God, then there is no hope. If it were out of passion, then it might pass away. Often you observe a man whose face is red and swollen with passion, but it passed away. But ah! God's wrath is not out of pas-sion. If it were out of passion, surely God would have some pity when he saw the sufferings of the lost for many ages; but ah! no. From what then does it proceed? It proceeds from the rectitude of God. If God can cease to love righteousness, then the fire may be quenched. But as long as he is a righteous God, that fire will never be quenched. Oh! brethren, it is a foolish hope you entertain that the fire will be quenched. I have seen some on their death-bed thinking that the fire may be quenched. Ah! it is a vain hope, sinner. God will never cease to be a righteous God. God will do anything to save a sinner, but he cannot part with his rectitude in order to save you. He parted with his Son in order that he might gain sinners, but he cannot part with his righteousness. He cannot part with his government. He would need to call good evil and evil good first.*

*Robert Murray McCheyne, 1813–1843*

❖  ❖  ❖

CONCLUSION: All mankind, both Jew and Gentile alike, deserve God's condemnation—Romans 3:9-20

So what am I saying? That we Jews have an edge on the Gentiles? Not entirely. For I have already brought the charge against both Jews and Gentiles alike that we are all living in the grip of sin. As it is written,

> *There is no one righteous, not even one;*
>     *there is no one who understands,*
>         *there is no one really seeking after the true God.*
> *Their interests have all turned away to other things,*
>     *together they have squandered their lives;*
> *there is no one who shows real kindness,*
>     *not so much as one.*

*Their speech exhales their inner moral rot;*
*    their words are meant to deceive.*
*Lying under the surface of their chatter is*
*    venomous intent.*
*Their speech is heavily laced with hostility*
*    and malice.*
*They are trigger-happy, running headlong*
*    into violence;*
*they leave a trail of destruction and sorrow wherever*
*    they go;*
*they have no concept of what it takes to live*
*    together in peace.*
*Basically, their view of God is so weak that they*
*    see no reason to restrain themselves.*

We realize, moreover, that all these Old Testament denunciations of human sin apply first to Jews, to whom they were first addressed. Far from implying that the Jews are better than others, their possession of God's law closes *every* mouth, it silences *every* whining excuse, both Jewish and Gentile. The whole human race, every one of us without exception, stands speechless in guilt before our holy Judge. No one's conformity to the demands of the law—the very thing upright people take pride in achieving—will ever win acquittal from God, for his law is intended not to provide sinners with the resources with which they may earn God's approval but just the opposite. His law is meant to confront us with our sinfulness. —Romans 3:9-20

**PRAYER**    O Lord God above, your law exposes and condemns *me*. When it denounces mankind, it points at *me*. At any given moment, I suppose, I may appear to be a fairly decent person. But when the light of your holy law searches and exposes the true inner movements of my soul, I too stand condemned. No amount of behavioral adjustment on my part, no depth of psychological self-mastery, can go down deep enough to remove or even control my sinfulness. Sin has marked my psyche, branded my soul, seared my conscience. And encouraging my sin is my insultingly impudent attitude toward you. I do not fear you. I treat you as if your promises were cheap and your threats were empty. So there is no way that I deserve your approval. I close my mouth and claim nothing from you as my due. For once in my life, O God, let me right now admit my guilt before you without evasion, without excuses, without blaming my circumstances or parents or anyone else. I sin because *I* am sinful. O holy God, I humble myself before you now and accept your dismal assessment of me as searchingly true and stingingly accurate. Have mercy upon me, a sinner. In the holy name of Christ. Amen.

> *Show me myself, O holy Lord;*
>    *Help me to look within.*
> *I will not turn me from the sight*
>    *Of all my sin.*
>
> *Just as it is in thy pure eyes*
>    *Would I behold my heart.*
> *Bring every hidden spot to light,*
>    *Nor shrink the smart.*
>
> *Not mine, the purity of heart*
>    *That shall at last see God.*
> *Not mine, the following in the steps*
>    *The Savior trod.*
>
> *Not mine, the life I thought to live*
>    *When first I took his name.*
> *Mine but the right to weep and grieve*
>    *Over my shame.*

*Yet, Lord, I thank thee for the sight*
*Thou hast vouchsafed to me.*
*And, humbled to the dust, I shrink*
*Closer to thee.*

*Thomas Pollock, 1836–1896*

❖ ❖ ❖

GOD'S ANSWER to our problem is the cross of Christ, the benefits of which we receive by faith—Romans 3:21-5:21

JESUS SATISFIED the righteous demands of God's law at the cross, opening the way for us into God's favor and demonstrating God's justice—Romans 3:21-26

But now, accepting that we stand condemned before God, we are finally prepared to hear the good news. God has revealed his way of declaring us righteous in his sight, and it has nothing to do with our earning his favor by keeping the law. His method of restoring sinners is no novelty, however. The law and the prophets teach it. What I am talking about is justification by faith in Jesus Christ, and it applies equally to all who receive his merit with the empty hands of faith. There is no ranking, no hierarchy, no distinction between people when it comes to justification, for we all have equally discredited ourselves by our sins. None of us is anywhere near coming up to God's glorious standard. This is why God reinstates us in his favor as a free gift. Our justification is all of his grace, paid for at the cross by Christ Jesus, whose death won our release from the moral debt we owed. God put Jesus there on the cross as the sacrificial Lamb placating God's holy wrath, justly offended at the outrage of our sins. Our part is simply to look upon his bloody sacrifice in faith. God had a point to make at that cross. He wanted us to know that he is a just Judge. He does not trivialize our sin. He hates it. For a long time he had patiently allowed human sin to accumulate unpunished. But at the cross God finally demonstrated that he does uphold a perfect moral standard. The cross, then, shows us this glorious paradox: God executes his justice against human sin *and* God justifies the one who trusts in Jesus.—Romans 3:21-26

**PRAYER** O God and Father, this is too profound for me to understand fully and yet too inviting for me to turn away. You do not forgive me by overlooking your law. Instead, the cross liberates your love by enforcing your law. Your justice has been satisfied. You have taken my guilt and put it onto Christ at the cross, where he suffered in my place the penalty my guilt deserved. And you have taken his righteousness and credited it to me, paying my moral debt in full forever. This mysterious exchange, my sin for his merit, is the wonder of free justification at the cross. O Father, how am I to respond? All I can do is bow before you in quiet adoration and wonder. O just Judge and gracious Savior, I do whisper my poor love back to you! Receive my worship now, for I offer it to you through the infinite merit of Christ. In his holy name. Amen.

> *Complete atonement thou hast made*
> *And to the utmost farthing paid whate'er thy*
> *people owed.*
> *How then can wrath on me take place,*
> *If sheltered in thy righteousness and sprinkled*
> *with thy blood?*
>
> *If thou hast my discharge procured*
> *And freely in my place endured the whole of*
> *wrath divine,*
> *Payment God cannot twice demand,*

First at my bleeding Surety's hand and then
again at mine.

Turn then, my soul, unto thy rest.
The merits of thy great High Priest speak peace
and liberty.
Trust in his efficacious blood,
Nor fear thy banishment from God, since Jesus
died for thee.

*Augustus Toplady, 1740–1778*

Now I saw in my dream, that the highway up which
Christian was to go was fenced on either side with a
wall, and that wall was called Salvation. Up this way,
therefore, did burdened Christian run, but not without
great difficulty because of the load on his back. He ran
thus till he came to a place somewhat ascending. And
upon that place stood a cross, and a little below, in the
bottom, a sepulchre. So I saw in my dream that just as
Christian came up to the cross, his burden loosed from
off his shoulders and fell from off his back and began
to tumble, and so continued to do till it came to the
mouth of the sepulchre, where it fell in, and I saw it no
more. Then was Christian glad and lightsome and said
with a merry heart, "He hath given me rest by His sorrow and life by His death." Then he stood still awhile
to look and wonder, for it was very surprising to him
that the sight of the cross should thus ease him of his
burden. He looked therefore and looked again, even till
the springs that were in his head sent the waters down
his cheeks.

*John Bunyan,* The Pilgrim's Progress, *1688*

❖   ❖   ❖

THE WAY OF FAITH invalidates all self-congratulatory pride
—Romans 3:27-31

> So what about our old feeling of moral superiority? It no
> longer has any place. For what reason? Because we failed
> to distinguish ourselves as upright people? No, for we
> managed that—at least outwardly. A self-congratulatory
> spirit has no place now because pride is incompatible
> with faith. We are convinced that we are justified by
> faith, quite apart from our compliance with God's law.
> So we reject all proud confidence in our own attainments
> and humbly trust in Christ alone. Or you could look at
> it this way. Is God limited to the Jews? Isn't he the God
> of the Gentiles as well? Yes, for there is only one God.
> Then that means he will justify both a Jew by faith and
> a Gentile by the same faith. One God, one justification.
> What does this mean, then, for his law? Do we end up
> cancelling the claims of the law by insisting on faith
> alone? Unthinkable! The gospel affirms the authority of
> God's moral law and, as we shall see, enables us truly to
> obey it.—Romans 3:27-31

PRAYER    O Lord, I used to cherish the most exquisite sense
that I was better than most people. It felt so good, perceiving
myself that way. It felt good, looking down on the immoral
masses from a position of superiority. I even looked down on
other Christians who failed to meet my particular standards of
acceptability. That feeling of superior virtue was delicious, but it
was also self-deceived. I repudiate it, Lord. I pour contempt on
it, for it demeans you. It demeans your cross. Now I embrace you
alone as my *only* legitimacy before God. You alone are my wisdom, righteousness, sanctification and redemption. You alone
are my narrow escape. Now, when I boast, let me boast only of
all that you are to me. In your holy name. Amen.

*Spiritual pride is the main door by which the devil comes into the hearts of those who are zealous for the advancement of religion. It is the chief inlet of smoke from the bottomless pit, to darken the mind and mislead the judgment. This is the main handle by which the devil has hold of religious persons, and the chief source of all the mischief that he introduces, to clog and hinder a work of God. . . . Alas! how much pride have the best of us in our hearts! It is the worst part of the body of sin and death, the first sin that ever entered into the universe and the last that is rooted out. It is God's most stubborn enemy!*

*Jonathan Edwards, 1703–1758*

# ROMANS

## CHAPTER 4

BIBLICAL PRECEDENT in Abraham confirms that justification by faith excludes all self-righteous pride—Romans 4:1-25

*The Old Testament teaches free justification—Romans 4:1-8*

But what about Abraham, the patriarch of God's people? What did he meet with in his relationship with God? If it is true that Abraham won his way into God's favor, then he really has something to boast about. But that is impossible. Nobody boasts before God. What, after all, does Scripture say? "Abraham put his faith in God, and his faith was credited to him as righteousness." And what does that verse teach us? It teaches us something about faith. When someone works to earn a wage, that wage is not credited to him as a favor but as an obligation. He has earned it. But suppose someone does not *work* to earn God's approval. Suppose someone only puts his *faith* in God, trusting God to reinstate him even though he has failed God. What then? It is only his faith that is credited to him as righteousness. He has not earned anything at all.

David, as well, illustrates this principle. Look at the way he describes the joy of the one to whom God imputes righteousness quite apart from his moral record:

> How glad are they
>   whose transgressions are forgiven,
>   whose sins are covered!
>
> How glad is the one
>   whose sin the Lord will never hold against him!

—Romans 4:1-8

**PRAYER**     O Lord, my natural religious instincts are so perverse that I might even twist faith into a reason for pride, but the light of your gospel illuminates my darkness. I do acknowledge that not even my faith deserves your favor. Only the merit of Christ deserves your favor. Nothing in my hand I bring—not even my faith; simply to your cross I cling. My new relationship with you is all of your grace, for my faith is not meritorious in value but only instrumental in function. My faith is merely the avenue along which you bestow mercy, not an invoice on which I demand payment. I therefore abandon *all* lingering sense of my own entitlement and open my heart to the joy of your free grace lavished upon me in Christ. Fill my heart, Lord, with the humble faith of Abraham and with the boundless joy of David, I pray. In the holy name of Christ. Amen.

> Not what I feel or do
>   Can give me peace with God.
> Not all my prayers and sighs and tears
>   Can bear my awful load.

> Thy work alone, O Christ,
>   Can ease this weight of sin.
> Thy blood alone, O Lamb of God,
>   Can give me peace within.

*Thy love to me, O God,*
*Not mine, O Lord, to thee,*
*Can rid me of this dark unrest*
*And set my spirit free.*

*I bless the Christ of God.*
*I rest on love divine.*
*And with unfaltering lip and heart*
*I call this Savior mine.*

*Horatius Bonar, 1808–1889*

❖  ❖  ❖

*Free justification is not limited to Jews but belongs to all believers everywhere, Jewish and Gentile, on the same basis*
*—Romans 4:9-12*

Now, is the gladness of justification that David speaks of meant for Jews only, or is it for Gentiles as well? For Gentiles as well, since my position is based on the fact that Abraham was put right with God by mere faith. Think about it. When Abraham was justified, was he circumcised or uncircumcised? He was uncircumcised. Years later he received the rite of circumcision as a symbol, certifying his justification by faith which had occurred while he was still uncircumcised. God ordered this sequence of events for a reason. He wanted to make Abraham the spiritual father even of Gentiles, so that righteousness could be credited to them. And God also wanted to make Abraham the spiritual father of those Jews who are not only marked by the rite of circumcision but who also live out the same faith that our father Abraham displayed while still uncircumcised. What God did in Abraham, then, shows that both Jews and Gentiles are justified in the same way—by faith.—Romans 4:9-12

**PRAYER**    O Father, all your children are one, for we all enter into Christ on the same terms. Red and yellow, black and white, all are precious in your sight, for we are all clothed with the righteousness of Christ. We are young and old, rich and poor, men and women. We belong to the Roman, Eastern and Protestant churches. And none of us has warrant for boasting pride of place. Our common faith prohibits all ranking of one over another when it comes to justification, for it is Another's righteousness, not our sectarian distinctives, which legitimates us in your sight. You, Lord Jesus Christ, are all our pride, and all who believe share you equally. Bind your holy catholic church together, O Lord, with the mutual respect that justification by faith alone logically entails. May we be one in faith and love. In your holy name. Amen.

> *[Arminian] John Wesley never encouraged criticism of [Calvinist] George Whitefield. "Do you think we shall see Mr. Whitefield in heaven?" asked one small-minded disciple. "No," replied Wesley, and the man looked pleased that he had aimed his flattery well. "No, sir," said Wesley, "I fear not. Mr. Whitefield will be so near the Throne and we at such a distance we shall hardly get a sight of him."*
>
> John Pollock, 1972

❖   ❖   ❖

*Free justification ensures that all believers will inherit God's covenant promises to them—Romans 4:13-17a*

God made a promise to Abraham (and to us, his children) that he would inherit the world under the full blessing of God. This promise was made to Abraham not on the condition that he would then earn a claim to it by obeying God's law but simply because he was right with God by faith. After all, if we have to qualify as heirs of the promise by keeping the law, faith is rendered meaningless and the promise is effectively cancelled. Why? Because, given what we are, a law-based relationship with God can only have the effect of bringing wrath down on our heads. But in a relationship where no merit can be earned, neither can the promise be lost. What we *deserve* is simply irrelevant. And here is the reason why our new relationship with God is a matter of faith. God wants it to be all of grace, so that there can be no uncertainty about the outcome. He wants us all to be confident that his promise stands firm and that we will inherit it. And this assurance is good for Jewish believers who continue to observe the religious customs of the law and, no less, for Gentile believers who have only the faith of Abraham. He is the spiritual father of us all. As it is written, "I have made you the father of many nations."—Romans 4:13-17a

**PRAYER**    Gracious Father, you know how weak I am. A burden of lifelong uncertainty would be too heavy for my poor faith to bear. You have not required me to bear it. You have given me your solemn assurance that my faith will not turn out to have been an enormous miscalculation. You have promised that the merit of Christ my Savior will compensate for all my sins, including the imperfections of my faith. You have guaranteed that I will see all my heart's desire granted through your promise. My faith finds rest in you, not because my faith is so full of faith, but because your grace supports even my weak faith with an unbreakable promise. Great is your faithfulness, O God my Father. I rest in you. In the holy name of Christ. Amen.

*God is our God to death, in death, and forever. All
things in the world will fail us: friends will fail us, all
comforts will fail us, life will fail us ere long. But this is
an everlasting covenant, which will not fail.*

Richard Sibbes, 1577–1635

✧   ✧   ✧

*Justifying faith is a bold confidence in God, as we see in Abraham
—Romans 4:17b-22*

But what does this justifying faith actually look like in real
life? Again, consider Abraham. He was so confident in
God's promise that he looked for God to give new life to
the dead. He looked for God to confer existence upon
things that did not yet exist. He defied the parameters of
what is humanly possible and looked in hope for God to
keep his promise, however unlikely its fulfillment may
have seemed. This is how he became the father of many
nations—as God had said, "So shall your descendants
be." Abraham took God's promise more seriously than all
the appearances and circumstances contradicting it. From
the perspective of this faith, he looked square in the face
of the facts: his own body, deadened with age (for he was
around 100 years old), and the deadness of Sarah's
womb. But when it came to God's promise, Abraham did
not hover between doubt and belief but was enabled to
believe with a strong faith. And the fact that God's word
alone was enough to sustain him brought honor to God.
Abraham was filled with confidence that what God had
promised he could also accomplish. And this is the kind
of faith that is credited for righteousness. *This* faith is justifying faith.—Romans 4:17b-22

**PRAYER**    O Lord, I do not want a veneer of mere religion. I
want faith. Mark my soul with this Abrahamic faith. When I feel

abandoned by you, give me this faith. When I am overwhelmed with my own sinfulness, give me this faith. When I lie down in death, give me this faith. Let me walk through life seeing your power above and beyond the doubtful circumstances, the uncertainties and the crises around me and within me. Let me, O God, live by true faith, enabling me especially to obey your hard commands. In the holy name of Christ. Amen.

> *Since all men acknowledge the power of God, Paul seems to say nothing out of the ordinary about Abraham's faith. But experience shows that one of the most difficult attainments is to ascribe to the power of God the honor of which it is worthy. There is no obstacle, however small and insignificant, which does not lead the flesh to suppose that the hand of God is restrained from accomplishing his work. The result is that, in the slightest possible trials, the promises of God slide away from us. As I have said, it is an undisputed fact that no one denies the omnipotence of God. But as soon as any obstacle is raised to impede the course of his promise, we degrade his power. We do not sufficiently exalt the power of God if we do not consider it greater than our weakness. Faith, therefore, ought not to look to our weakness, misery and defects, but should fix its whole attention on the power of God alone.*
>
> *John Calvin, 1509–1564*

❖   ❖   ❖

*Abraham's faith is the model of all justifying faith*
*—Romans 4:23-25*

The relevance of this goes far beyond Abraham. Those biblical words, "It was credited to him," are not meant to describe merely an isolated episode in the life of a long-gone historical figure. We too are credited with righteousness, for we have put our trust in God who raised Jesus our Lord from the dead. He was handed over to death because we had sinned, and he was raised up to life again because his sacrifice had won our justification. —Romans 4:23-25

**PRAYER**  O Father, I take my stand with Abraham. I embrace your life-giving power and promise as my own. I trust you now and forever. I join all the others who have taken this step of faith—the great names along with the millions of unknown believers whose imperfect lives have nevertheless shown confidence in God amid the surrounding despair. Lord, I believe. Let my life show it. In the holy name of Christ. Amen.

> *Father of Jesus Christ, my Lord,*
> *My Savior and my Head,*
> *I trust in thee, whose powerful word*
> *Hath raised him from the dead.*
>
> *In hope, against all human hope,*
> *Self-desperate, I believe.*
> *Thy quickening word shall raise me up,*
> *Thou shalt thy Spirit give.*
>
> *Faith, mighty faith, the promise sees,*
> *And looks to that alone,*
> *Laughs at impossibilities*
> *And cries, It shall be done!*
>
> *Charles Wesley, 1707–1788*

# ROMANS

## CHAPTER 5

JUSTIFICATION BY FAITH opens up to us a new life of friendship
with God and assures us of a glorious salvation still to come
—Romans 5:1-11

So now that we have been justified by faith, what difference does it make in our lives? For one thing, we have
peace with God through our Lord Jesus Christ. Through
him we have been admitted by faith into the favored
position with God that we now occupy. Moreover, we
stand tall with the confidence that we will be made glorious with a perfection like God's own glory. And not
only that, but we hold our heads high even in our sufferings. We know that God uses our sufferings to produce in us endurance. The fact that we endure under
adversity, in turn, authenticates our faith. This proving
of our faith, in turn, encourages our confidence that we
really are destined for glory. Putting all our hopes in the
promise of the gospel will not prove, after all, to have
been a terrible mistake, because God's love for us has
flooded our hearts in the person of the Holy Spirit, who
has been given to us to lead us to glory.—Romans 5:1-5

**PRAYER**     Father in heaven, you have thought of everything. Justification, sanctification, glorification—you provide it all in a great outpouring of your mercy. No more tormented uncertainty as to where I stand with you! I enjoy the quiet assurance of your acceptance, for I have been justified through Christ. Your Holy Spirit has been poured into my heart to sanctify me with true holiness of life. And now I relish the thought of my heavenly inheritance—the glory of perfect Christlikeness. Not forever will I shame myself and degrade myself with my sins. Not forever will I agonize in self-loathing over my sins. Not forever will sin be the whip that keeps me in line. The Holy Spirit has come into my heart as a gift of your love, and he will accomplish your purpose in me. Speed the day, O Lord, when I will stand before you complete, lost in wonder, love and praise. In the holy name of Christ. Amen.

*In the battle of Waterloo, it was long thought that the French had gained, and Napoleon sent several dispatches to Paris telling that he had won. But in the fight with the world, Satan and the flesh, we know how the victory is to turn already. Christ has engaged to carry us through. He will guard us against the darts of the law by hiding us in his blood. He defends us from the power of sin by his Holy Spirit, put within us. . . . The thicker the battle, the closer he will keep to us. . . . Though the world were a million times more enraged, though the fires of persecution were again kindled, though my heart were a million times more wicked, though all the temptations of hell were let loose upon me, I know I shall overcome through him that loved me. . . . If God has chosen you, called you, washed you, justified you, then he will glorify you. O yield to his loving hands!*

*Robert Murray McCheyne, 1813–1843*

✧ ✧ ✧

And what is the nature of God's love for us? His love is unconditional and, therefore, inexhaustible. While we were still morally helpless—cold, indifferent, sullen— Christ came, on schedule and without reluctance, to die for ungodly people like us. Now, it is unlikely that one would willingly be a martyr for a just man, although perhaps one might dare to sacrifice oneself for a truly good man. But that is as far as our human love is willing to go. By contrast, God shows that his love for us is of another order entirely. While we were still sinners, Christ died for us. So then, if we have been restored to God's favor through Christ's blood, how much more certain is it that we will be fully saved by him from God's wrath! After all, if, alienated from him as we were, God broke down the barriers by the death of his Son, how much more certain is it, now that we are back on good terms with him, that we will be fully saved as he imparts his life to us! Our sins cannot jeopardize our full salvation, you see, because God's unconditional love for us has anticipated and compensated for those very sins. —Romans 5:6-10

PRAYER    O God, your love has already factored in all my resistance to your love. My hope, therefore, cannot be subverted by my own failure to live worthily of that hope. I am eternally secure in your overwhelming love. My thirst for glory will not be denied. I will inherit the fullness of salvation. And this is in no way whatsoever attributable to my initiative or worth. Your love has borne all the burden and compensated for all my failures with your grace. Receive my unworthy love in return right now, O loving Lord, as the assurance of the gospel makes its full claim upon my loyalties, for Jesus Christ's sake. In his holy name. Amen.

*Love bade me welcome, yet my soul drew back,*
   *Guilty of dust and sin.*
*But quick-eyed Love, observing me grow slack*
   *From my first entrance in,*
*Drew nearer to me, sweetly questioning*
   *If I lacked anything.*

*"A guest," I answered, "worthy to be here."*
   *Love said, "You shall be he."*
*"I, the unkind, ungrateful? Ah my dear,*
   *I cannot look on Thee."*
*Love took my hand and smiling did reply,*
   *"Who made the eyes but I?"*

*"Truth, Lord, but I have marred them; let my shame*
   *Go where it doth deserve."*
*"And know you not," says Love, "who bore the blame?"*
   *"My dear, then I will serve."*
*"You must sit down," says Love, "and taste my meat."*
   *So I did sit and eat.*

*George Herbert, 1593–1633*

❖ ❖ ❖

And not only that, but we also find in God himself another
reason for boasting. Through our Lord Jesus Christ we
have entered into a new relationship of nearness and
friendship with no one less than *God.*—Romans 5:11

**PRAYER**    O God, to have the Almighty Sovereign of the universe as my personal, watchful, caring friend, hovering over me,
showering daily graces upon me—this changes everything. In
your infinite perfection, you are sufficient for all my needs, now
and forever. Your love will never abandon me, even when I sin.
Your plan will never fail me, even when I lose my way. Your

sovereignty will never unthrone itself, allowing the enemies of my soul to rob me of your promises. All is well, for you are there, and you are mine. I boast in you, mighty Friend. In the holy name of Christ. Amen.

> *My God, my Life, my Love,*
>   *To thee, to thee I call.*
> *I cannot live, if thou remove,*
>   *For thou art all in all.*
>
> *Thy shining grace can cheer*
>   *This dungeon where I dwell.*
> *'Tis paradise when thou art here.*
>   *If thou depart, 'tis hell.*
>
> *Thou art the sea of love,*
>   *Where all my pleasures roll,*
> *The circle where my passions move*
>   *And center of my soul.*
>
> *To thee my spirits fly*
>   *With infinite desire.*
> *And yet how far from thee I lie—*
>   *Dear Jesus, raise me higher!*
>
> *Isaac Watts, 1674–1748*

✧ ✧ ✧

CONCLUSION: We are condemned because of what Adam did, but we are justified because of what Christ did—Romans 5:12-21

I want to emphasize the centrality of Christ in the gospel by drawing an analogy between Adam and Christ. Sin gained access to the human race through one man, Adam, with death following close behind. This explains

why the whole human race lies under a sentence of
death. Everyone sinned in Adam. Sin was active in the
world long before God revealed his law at Mount Sinai.
But sin is not registered in God's accounts as a violation
of his law, worthy of death, unless he has openly revealed
a prohibition for us to break. But the death penalty ruled
from Adam to Moses anyway, even though people did
not personally sin in the same way Adam did (namely,
in flagrant violation of God's revealed law), because
*in Adam* we did break God's clearly stated moral law.
—Romans 5:12-14a

**PRAYER**    O divine Physician, your diagnosis of my condition
is so much more profound than my own analysis of myself. I
would see myself as a wilted rose in need only of a generous
watering. You explain to me that, in fact, I am hemlock, growing vigorously in a world infested with hemlock, all from one
common root. My problem is not superficial. My problem is not
a little lie here or a lustful thought there. My problem is not even
a huge, shocking lie here and actual adultery there. My real problem underlies all the surface manifestations of my sin, and it is
the guilt and corruption of my very nature as a child of Adam.
O God, your gospel takes me deep, deep down, all the way to the
very root of my condemnation, all the way back to Adam. Now,
O Lord, lift me up, very, very high into the richness of your grace
in Christ, my Lord and Head. In his holy name. Amen.

> *Once more, behold, disquiet! Behold, once more sor-*
> *row and mourning confront him who seeks joy and*
> *gladness! My soul had begun in hope for fulfillment,*
> *and behold, it is again overwhelmed by poverty! I*
> *sought for nourishment, and behold, I begin to hunger*
> *more than before! I was striving to rise up to the light*
> *of God, and I fell back into my own darkness. Indeed,*
> *I not only fell into it, but I feel myself enveloped in it.*

*Before my mother conceived me, I fell. In truth, I was conceived in that darkness, and I was born wrapped up in it. In truth, we all fell long ago in him, in whom we all have sinned. In him we all have lost what he easily held and wickedly lost for himself and for us. Now, when we wish to seek it, we do not know it, and when we seek we do not find it, and what we find is not what we are seeking. Do help me for your goodness' sake, O Lord. I have sought your face, O Lord; your face will I search for. Turn not your face from me. Lift me up from myself to yourself. Cleanse, heal, sharpen, enlighten the eye of my mind, that it may behold you. Let my soul gather up her powers and with all her understanding reach out again to you, O Lord.*

*Anselm, ca. 1033–1109*

❖   ❖   ❖

Now Adam, as an individual crucial to the destiny of his descendants, prefigured the coming Christ, for our Lord likewise is crucial to the destiny of his followers. But the analogy breaks down at this point, because Adam's sin and Christ's gift cannot be evenly compared. If one man's act of sin doomed the many, how much more bountifully did God's grace pour out upon the many, bringing them the free gift of justification through the one man Jesus Christ! So Christ's grace far surpassed Adam's sin. And neither can the result of Adam's sin be compared with what Christ has done. God's judgment of us, resulting in our condemnation, originated in just one sin. But Christ's gift, resulting in our justification, compensated for many sins. His mercy toward us is out of all proportion to the original provocation. Moreover, Christ not only delivers from death but also imparts eternal life. For if, as a result of one man's sin, a death sentence claimed every human

life, how much more will those who receive abundant
grace in the gift of justification reign forever in eternal life
through the one man Jesus Christ!—Romans 5:14b-17

**PRAYER**    O Lord Jesus Christ, my Head, deepen my sense of
connection with you. When I fall into sin, show me the greater
grace of your cross. When my conscience writhes in pain, soothe
me with your all-covering righteousness. And when I cherish feelings of self-sufficiency, drifting away from you, call me back.
Renew the sweetness of felt union with you. I take you, Lord, as
all my sufficiency. If I have you, I have everything worth having,
whatever else I may lack. If I do not have you, I have nothing
worth having, whatever else I may possess. Cut me off from my
old, natural life in Adam. Unite me with yourself by the miracle
of grace, I pray, and make your perfect obedience mine as I stand
before God now and forever. In your holy name. Amen.

> *"Man," says the law of God, "have you obeyed my
> commands?"*
>
> *"No," says the sinner saved by grace. "I have dis-
> obeyed them, not only in the person of my representa-
> tive Adam in his first sin, but also in that I myself have
> sinned in thought, word and deed."*
>
> *"Well, then, sinner," says the law of God, "have you paid
> the penalty which I pronounced upon disobedience?"*
>
> *"No," says the sinner, "I have not paid the penalty
> myself. But Christ has paid it for me. He was my repre-
> sentative when he died there on the cross. Hence, so far
> as the penalty is concerned, I am clear."*
>
> *"Well, then, sinner," says the law of God, "how about
> the conditions which God has pronounced for the*

*attainment of assured blessedness? Have you stood the*
*test? Have you merited eternal life by perfect obedience*
*during the period of probation?"*

*"No," says the sinner, "I have not merited eternal life*
*by my own perfect obedience. God knows and my own*
*conscience knows that even after I became a Christian*
*I have sinned in thought, word and deed. But although*
*I have not merited eternal life by any obedience of my*
*own, Christ has merited it for me by his perfect obedi-*
*ence. He was not for himself subject to the law. No*
*obedience was required of him for himself, since he*
*was Lord of all. That obedience, then, which he ren-*
*dered to the law when he was on earth was rendered*
*by him as my representative. I have no righteousness of*
*my own, but clad in Christ's perfect righteousness,*
*imputed to me and received by faith alone, I can glory*
*in the fact that, so far as I am concerned, the probation*
*has been kept and, as God is true, there awaits me the*
*glorious reward which Christ thus earned for me."*

*J. Gresham Machen, 1881–1937*

❖ ❖ ❖

So then, just as condemnation has fallen upon us all
through the sin of Adam, so also justification, guaranteeing eternal life, has come to us all through the righteousness of Christ. For as the disobedience of the one
man made the many sinners, the obedience of the other
man will make the many right with God. The law of
Moses eventually came along, but not as the solution to
our sin problem. Rather, the law aroused our inclination
to sin even further. But that did not defeat God. For
where sin multiplied, grace over-multiplied. God has
provided an excess of grace to overmatch our sin. So just
as sin once reigned over us, condemning us to death, so

now grace reigns supreme through justification, guaranteeing us eternal life, through Jesus Christ our Lord. We see then that grace, not law, has triumphed over sin, and that Christ, not Moses, is our Savior.—Romans 5:18-21

**PRAYER**    O God, human theories as to what is wrong with the world and how to fix it are both unnecessarily complex and, at the same time, thin and trite. But your explanation is simple, clear and true. There is Adam, and there is Christ. In Adam, I have a problem—sin and death. In Christ, I have a solution—justification and life. And his gracious solution far outweighs my sinful problem. I will never exhaust the resources of my new Head, with whom I live in deep union forever. When I repent of the very worst sin I will ever commit, I will not find that I have gone beyond the depth of his mercy. No pit of my sin can go deeper than his grace. O God, I do receive Jesus now. I joyfully affirm his headship over me and his grace cleansing me. Reign in grace, Lord Jesus! Let my life be a living demonstration that your grace breaks the degrading power of sin. In your holy name. Amen.

*I can feelingly say, he hath proved himself stronger than I and his goodness superior to all my unworthiness. He tells me (and enables me to believe it) that I am fair, and there is no spot in me. Though an enemy, he calls me his friend; though a traitor, a child; though a beggared prodigal, he clothes me with the best robe and has put a ring of endless love and mercy on my hand. And though I am sorely distressed by spiritual and internal foes, afflicted, tormented and bowed down almost to death with the sense of my own present barrenness, ingratitude and proneness to evil, he secretly shows me his bleeding wounds and softly and powerfully whispers to my soul, "I am thy great salvation." His free distinguishing grace is the bottom on which is fixed the rest of my poor weary tempted soul. On this I ground my hope, often times when unsupported by any other evidence, save only the Spirit of adoption received from him. When my dry and empty barren soul is parched with thirst, he kindly bids me come to him and drink my fill at the fountain head. In a word, he empowers me to say with experiential evidence, "Where sin abounded, grace did much more abound." Amen and Amen.*

Joseph Hart, 1712-1768

# ROMANS

## CHAPTER 6

### THE CLARIFICATION OF THE GOSPEL—ROMANS 6:1-11:36

BY PROMISING A SURPLUS of grace for sinners, does the gospel throw open the door to more and more sinning, so that grace may shine all the more brightly? No, because grace unites us with Christ in his death, burial and resurrection—Romans 6:1-14

What then should we infer from this gospel of plentiful grace? We have seen that God justifies us not by our obedience but by his grace. Indeed, the more we have sinned, the more grace God has showered upon us in our justification. So does this gospel teach us to go on sinning, so that we may give grace its maximum opportunity? Unthinkable! Our conversion to grace entailed our *dying* to sin. So how could we go on as if nothing has changed? Everything has changed! Or don't you realize that whoever is baptized into Christ Jesus, as we have been, is baptized into his death? Through baptism we were buried, as Christ was buried, stone dead. Our old life is *over*. And the whole point of our union with Christ in his death and burial is that, just as he was raised from the dead by the glorious power of the Father, we too should begin living a new life. If we have been united with him in this kind of death, we must surely rise again with him in a new way of life.—Romans 6:1-5

**PRAYER** O my Lord, how can I live a morally indifferent life, as if little has changed? Grace forbids it, because the life of grace is a life of profound spiritual union with you, my crucified, buried and risen Head. You have taught me to expect new holiness to emerge from within my character, for the life of grace includes sanctification no less than justification. After all, you rose just as much as you died and were buried. So how could your grace fail to lift me to a new life? O risen Lord, raise me up in newness of life. Let my justification bear fruit in sanctification. Make your grace, for me, not an excuse for sin but a power for obedience, I earnestly pray. In your holy name. Amen.

*What does Paul do? He takes this great truth of our acceptance in Christ our Merit and puts it unreserved, unrelieved, unspoiled, in contact with other truth of coordinate, nay, of superior greatness, for it is the truth to which justification leads us, as way to end. He places our acceptance through Christ Atoning in organic connection with our life in Christ Risen. . . . Justification has indeed set the sinner free from the condemning claim of sin, from guilt. He is as if he had died the death of sacrifice, oblation and satisfaction; as if he had passed through the Lama Sabachthani, and had "poured out his soul" for sin. . . . But then, because he thus died "in Christ," he is "in Christ" still, in respect also of resurrection. He is justified, not that he may go away, but that in his Justifier he may live with the pow-*

*ers of that holy and eternal life with which the Justifier
rose again. The two truths are concentrated as it were
into one by their equal relation to the same Person, the
Lord. The previous argument has made us intensely
conscious that justification, while a definite transaction
in law, is not a mere transaction. It lives and glows
with the truth of connection with a Person. That
Person is the Bearer for us of all merit. But He is also
and equally the Bearer for us of new life, in which the
sharers of His merit share, for they are in Him. So,
while the way of Justification can be isolated for study,
as it has been in this Epistle, the justified man cannot
be isolated from Christ, who is his life. And thus he can
never ultimately be considered apart from his possession in Christ of a new possibility, a new power, a new
and glorious call to living holiness. . . . Because we are
justified, we are to be holy, separated from sin, separated to God, not as a mere indication that our faith is
real, and that therefore we are legally safe, but because
we were justified for this very purpose, that we might
be holy. . . . It is a thing not to be thought of that the
sinner should accept justification—and live to himself.
It is a moral contradiction of the very deepest kind and
cannot be entertained without betraying an initial error
in the man's whole spiritual creed.*

*H. C. G. Moule, 1841–1920*

❖  ❖  ❖

We must understand that our old self, our natural bent
so congenial with sin—that old self has been *crucified*
with Christ. That is, when we came by faith to the cross,
we renounced our past and left it hanging up there on the
cross, where Christ our Head bore its guilt for us. Our
sinful self was decisively defeated there, so that slavery to

sin would no longer set the direction and tone of our lives, for anyone who has died with Christ has been justified and thus released from sin's enfeebling burden. And if we have died with Christ to our old life, we are convinced that we will also live with him in a new life. That stands to reason, for Christ, now that he is raised from the dead, can never die again. Death has no hold on him anymore. For the death he died, he died to defeat sin once and for all. But the life he is living now, he lives triumphantly for God. And my point is this: The gospel teaches you to see your own lives in union with Christ's death and resurrection. Your conversion was your death with Christ to the old life, bringing that era to a close. Now your ongoing faith is a fresh beginning in Christ, to the glory of God. So grace does not invite us to match its abundance with all the more sin, but the opposite. Grace teaches us to leave sin behind and follow Christ into a new life devoted to God.—Romans 6:6-11

**PRAYER**    O God, we your church are losing our radical edge, because we have forgotten this aspect of the gospel. Our discipleship is so flimsy, so unconvincing, because we do not understand this basic doctrine of death to sin, followed by new life, in union with our crucified, buried and risen Lord. We do not see our conversion to Christ as a death to our old life. We see it as a pleasant ornament on our old life—a little religion added in. We see conversion as a drop of oil to keep the gears of our pagan lives running smoothly, when in fact conversion demands that the gears come to a stop and begin turning in the opposite direction. We condescend to *include* you in our unexamined lives rather than *die* to those old lives and start all over again with you from scratch. O God, we urgently need to understand what you are teaching us here. We need to rediscover what it means to live in union with Christ. We need to see that holiness is not legalism and that grace is not cheap. O God, spread this message throughout your church today. Let it reach our ears and our hearts, creating within us a yearning for renewal in holiness, consistent with the gospel. And, O God, let me live in sweet, felt union with my Lord, drawing new life from him moment by moment. In his holy name. Amen.

*The tree of life my soul hath seen,*
*Laden with fruit and always green;*
*The trees of nature fruitless be,*
*Compared with Christ the apple tree.*

*His beauty doth all things excel;*
*By faith I know, but ne'er can tell*
*The glory which I now can see*
*In Jesus Christ the apple tree.*

*For happiness I long have sought,*
*And pleasure dearly I have bought;*
*I missed of all; but now I see*
*'Tis found in Christ the apple tree.*

*I'm weary with my former toil;*
*Here I will sit and rest a while,*
*Under the shadow I will be*
*Of Jesus Christ the apple tree.*

*I'll sit and eat this fruit divine,*
*It cheers my heart like spiritual wine;*
*And now this fruit is sweet to me,*
*That grows on Christ the apple tree.*

*This fruit doth make my soul to thrive;*
*It keeps my dying faith alive;*
*Which makes my soul in haste to be*
*With Jesus Christ the apple tree.*

*Anonymous, New Hampshire, 1761*

✧   ✧   ✧

So you can see that grace calls you to fight sin's desire to dominate your life. Do not let its passions control you. Do not make yourselves, in all your various capacities, available to sin as tools of wickedness. On the contrary, offer yourselves wholly to God as ones newly alive, with all your capacities as weapons of righteousness for God. The sin within you is doomed. It is not your destiny to live forever under its power, for you are no longer under the condemnation of the law but are now under the promise of grace.—Romans 6:12-14

**PRAYER**    O Savior, how glorious it will be to live in complete abandonment to your will. To be totally devoted to you, right down to my deepest impulses, to be *incapable* of betraying you, to find love and joy and purity flowing out of me—this is what I was made for and what I long for. And this is what you have promised I will become, by your grace. Whatever it takes, Lord, whatever loss I must suffer to gain the life that is truly life, I bow to the surgery of grace in my soul. In your holy name. Amen.

*Cheap grace means grace sold on the market like cheap-jack's wares. The sacraments, the forgiveness of sin, and the consolations of religion are thrown away at cut prices. Grace is represented as the church's inexhaustible treasury, from which she showers blessings with generous hands, without asking questions or fixing limits. . . . Grace alone does everything, they say, and so everything can remain as it was before. . . . That is what we mean by cheap grace, the grace which amounts to the justification of sin without the justification of the repentant sinner who departs from sin and from whom sin departs. . . . Cheap grace is the preaching of forgiveness without requiring repentance, baptism without church discipline,*

*communion without confession, absolution without per-
sonal confession. Cheap grace is grace without discipleship, grace without the cross, grace without Jesus Christ,
living and incarnate. Costly grace is the treasure hidden in
the field; for the sake of it a man will gladly go and sell all
that he has. It is the pearl of great price, to buy which the
merchant will sell all his goods. It is the kingly rule of
Christ, for whose sake a man will pluck out the eye
which causes him to stumble; it is the call of Jesus Christ
at which the disciple leaves his nets and follows him.*

*Dietrich Bonhoeffer, 1937*

❖  ❖  ❖

BUT IF THE GOSPEL of abundant grace does not *encourage* sinning,
does it still *allow* a casual attitude toward sin? No, because the
gospel affirms that slavery to sin breeds death, while slavery to
righteousness nurtures life—Romans 6:15-23

> So where does that leave us? May we still indulge in sin
> because the threat of the law has been lifted and grace
> is always there to forgive us? Does the doctrine of grace
> mean that now we can take sin less seriously?
> Unthinkable! Don't you realize that you always end up
> serving the one to whom you offer yourselves? Offer
> yourselves to sin, and your existence becomes a living
> death. Offer yourselves to obedience, and you grow into
> righteousness. Your choices have consequences. But,
> thank the Lord, although you once were slaves to sin,
> you have submitted fully to the new theological under-
> standing you have been taught.—Romans 6:15-17

PRAYER   O Lord, your grace does not set me free to do
whatever I please. Your grace frees me to live in obedience to
you. Free I am; freed I am not. I am free from condemnation and

eternal hell, but I am not freed from the practical consequences of my moment-by-moment decisions. Lord, I know too well the bitter fruit of sinful indulgence—the vindictive word, the incautious act, the hateful thought, how they breed sorrow, regret, remorse, shame, self-hatred, and still more sin. The world, the flesh and the devil argue strenuously and deceitfully that sin bears no consequences. "You will not die," they always tell me. They toss out the bait, but they hide the hook. They lie. And sometimes I choose to believe them, taking hypocritical advantage of your grace. But I am learning that your grace does not shield me from the practical results of my sins. And thus you have given me a powerful incentive to fear you even as I trust you, to run from sin even as I cling to justification. O Lord, keep a hedge about me today. Keep me from sin today. Enable me to walk in the strict disciplines of obedience, that I might enjoy the sweet taste of holiness. In the holy name of Christ. Amen.

*That seeming sweet that is in sin will quickly vanish, and lasting shame, sorrow, horror and terror will come in the room thereof. . . . Many long to be meddling with the murdering morsels of sin, which nourish not but rend and consume the belly, the soul that receives them. Many eat on earth what they digest in hell. Sin's murdering morsels will deceive those that devour them. Adam's apple was a bitter sweet. Esau's mess was a bitter sweet. The Israelites' quails a bitter sweet. Jonathan's honey a bitter sweet. And Adonijah's dainties a bitter sweet. After the meal is ended, then comes the reckoning.*

*Thomas Brooks, 1608–1680*

❖   ❖   ❖

**Now that you have been freed from slavery to sin, you have been bound over to serve a new master, righ-**

teousness. (I apologize for using the unworthy analogy of slavery, but it is easy to forget that God's grace demands our obedience.) Accordingly, just as you used to give yourselves as slaves to filthy living and moral chaos, with more and more chaos as the result, now dedicate everything you are, your every capacity, to serving righteousness, with growing personal holiness as the result. After all, when you were in the service of sin, you did whatever you felt like doing, heedless of righteousness. But what did you gain by living that way? It pains you even to recall those episodes! Why? Because the consequence of such behavior is a living death. But now, everything has changed. You have been freed from old master Sin and enslaved to a new master, God. And what you are getting out of your new service is an emerging holiness, the outcome of which is life eternal. For the wage sin pays is death. But the gift God gives is the richness and fullness of life in Christ Jesus our Lord. So do you really want to sip the poison of sin, when there is rich joy in obeying Christ?
—Romans 6:18-23

**PRAYER** Master and Lord, you have given me no choice. If I want to be a Christian at all, I must serve you with a holy life. This is non-negotiable. So, how may I enslave myself more fully, more particularly, to you? How may my obedience be made more precise, more thorough? Put your finger on definite attitudes, habits, perceptions, feelings and desires which displease you. Identify them for me and root them out of me. I cannot take my sins to heaven with me, and I have little time now to become holy. My soul is of infinite worth. My obligation to you is absolute. So let me work out my salvation, as you work in me. Take my sins, one by one, and build a new me out of the wreckage I offer you. I open my heart to you now. In the holy name of Christ. Amen.

*Revered and much respected,*

*Grace, mercy and peace be to you. I long to hear how
your soul prospereth, and I expected you would have
written to me. My earnest desire to you is that you
would seek the Lord and his face. I know that you are
not ignorant that your daylight is going fast away, and
your sun is declining. I beseech you by the mercies of
God and by the wounds of your redeeming Lord and
your dreadful appearance before the awesome Judge of
quick and dead, make your account clear and plain
with your Judge and Lord while ye have fair daylight,
for your night is coming on. Therefore, I pray you,
judge more of the worth of your soul. Know that if you
are in Christ, and secure your own soul, you are
blessed forever. Few, few, yea very few are saved. Grace
is not casten down at every man's door. Therefore,
speed yourself and others upon seeking Christ and salvation. Learn to overcome, in the bitterness of your
soul, your sins in time. It is not easy to take heaven, as
the Word saith, "by violence." Keep your tongue from
cursing and swearing. Refrain from wrath and malice.
Forgive all men for Christ's sake, as you would have
your Lord forgive you. I pray you, seeing your time is
short, make speed in your journey to heaven, that you
may secure a lodging to your soul against night.*

*Remember my love to your wife, William your son,
and the rest of your children. Grace be with you.*

> *Yours, at all hours, in Christ,*
> *S.R.*
> *Aberdeen, January 5, 1638*
>
> *Samuel Rutherford, 1600–1661*
> *writing from prison to Thomas MacCulloch*

# ROMANS
## CHAPTER 7

MOREOVER, THE THREAT of the law's condemnation does not deter sin. It only bonds us more firmly to our sin—Romans 7:1-6

But let me clarify something. The question raised in 6:15 about God's grace—that grace strips us of any incentive not to sin—that question itself is wrong to begin with. It assumes that we *need* the threat of the law's condemnation to make us obey God. But that kind of relationship with the law is itself a part of our old life. Don't you realize, dear friends—for you know the law—that a law-based relationship with God governs a person only as long as he continues in the *old* life? Let me illustrate. By law, a married woman is obliged to remain faithful to her husband as long as he lives. If he dies, she is released from her legal obligation to him. So then, if she gives herself to another man while her husband remains alive, she will be stigmatized as an adulteress. But if her husband dies, she is free from that law, so that marrying a new husband does not make her an adulteress. And here is my point, dear friends: You are like that woman, your old self is like that first husband, and the threat of condemnation once held the marriage together. It was your only incentive for faithfulness. But through the cross of Christ you have died. The old marriage is over, and you are beyond the law's power to condemn. You have a new husband, one who was raised from the dead, so that you would bear the fruit of holiness for God. Union with Christ, therefore, gives you incentives other than fear of condemnation for obeying God's law.—Romans 7:1-4

**PRAYER**    O dear Lord, I would never have taken this risk. If I had been the Savior, I would have kept the threat of eternal condemnation hanging over the heads of my people until they were safe in heaven. I would have kept them constantly off-balance, always uncertain. I would have exploited their fear of damnation as the whip to keep them in line. But your grace and wisdom are far superior to mine and your resources far richer. All I can do is threaten. But by your Spirit, you can indwell. You can renew. You can impart a joyful love for holiness. Teach *me*, Spirit of Christ, who I am and whose I am. Teach me what it means to live in vital union with my crucified, buried and risen Head. Let me leave the past behind and move on to new things with him. Let me obey your law out of gladness rather than dread. O Holy Spirit, put your glorious life deep down within me and mark me as Christ's forever. In his holy name. Amen.

> *Christ hath freed you from all your enemies, from the curse of the law, the predominant damnatory power of sin, the wrath of God, the sting of death and the torments of hell. But what is the end and design of Christ in doing these great and marvelous things for his people? It is not that we should throw off duties of righteousness and holiness, but that our hearts may be the more free and sweet in all holy duties and heavenly services. . . . Ah, souls! I know no such arguments to work you to a lively and constant performance of all*

*heavenly services like those that are drawn from the consideration of the great and glorious things that Christ hath done for you. And if such arguments will not take you and win you over, I do think the throwing of hell fire in your faces will never do it.*

*Thomas Brooks, 1608–1680*

❖ ❖ ❖

Let me explain further. In our old life, the law did not curb our sinful impulses. Just the opposite. They were aggravated all the more by the confinements imposed and penalties threatened by the law. Even as we tried to obey God's commandments, our evil inclinations were highly active in every aspect of our beings. The net result was not moral restraint but an explosion of even more sin, plunging us ever deeper into death. But now we have been released from the law's condemnation. We have died to that old self-defeating approach to the law in which we were held captive. Now we obey God out of a new spiritual power within and not by the old method of merely outward compliance with biblical commands. The law's threat of condemnation, therefore, is not what restrains sin. God's grace must do that deep within our hearts.—Romans 7:5-6

**PRAYER** O Lord, it is true. I need more than your law. I need more than instructions. I need more than challenge. I need even more than fear of punishment. I need *enablement*. I need a new power, a new nature within. I need renewal. O living Lord, copy your holy law from the pages of the Bible onto the tablet of my heart. Let me see your holiness appear, by grace, from within me, as you fill me full of your Spirit. Lord, I surrender myself to your spiritual surgery. Come and do a new work in me, I pray. In the holy name of Christ. Amen.

*O for a heart to praise my God,*
*A heart from sin set free,*
*A heart that's sprinkled with the blood*
*So freely shed for me.*

*A heart resigned, submissive, meek,*
*My great Redeemer's throne,*
*Where only Christ is heard to speak,*
*Where Jesus reigns alone.*

*A humble, lowly, contrite heart,*
*Believing, true and clean,*
*Which neither life nor death can part*
*From him that dwells within.*

*A heart in every thought renewed*
*And full of love divine,*
*Perfect and right and pure and good—*
*A copy, Lord, of thine.*

*Thy nature, gracious Lord, impart.*
*Come quickly from above.*
*Write thy new name upon my heart,*
*Thy new, best name of love.*

                          Charles Wesley, 1707–1788

❖   ❖   ❖

BUT IF THE LAW stirs up my sinfulness, then is the law to blame
for my condition? No. My problem is my own sinful nature,
which the law exposes to plain view—Romans 7:7-25

What then should we think of God's law? Is it evil?
Unthinkable! But I had no insight into sin until I tried
to meet the challenge of the law. For example, I could

not have understood how deeply self-centered I am except as the tenth commandment told me, "You must not envy." But sin, getting a foothold by that prohibition, reacted against the commandment and prompted within me all kinds of envious feelings. (In the absence of the law sin is dead, lacking an excuse for aggression.) There was a time, before I encountered the law, when I lived with an easy conscience. But when I came face to face with God's moral expectations revealed in the law, sin exploded with fresh life and I brought death upon myself. The very commandment that pointed the way to life proved, in my case, to result in death. For it was sin that got a foothold in me through the commandment and deceived me into thinking I could obey God on my own. Through the law, then, sin killed my complacent naiveté. So is the law evil? No! The law is holy, and each of its commandments is holy and just and good.
—Romans 7:7-12

*Question 147: What are the duties required by the tenth commandment?*

*Answer: The duties required by the tenth commandment are such contentment with our lot in life and such generosity of heart toward others that all our emotions are predisposed favorably toward others' true interests.*

*Question 148: What are the sins forbidden by the tenth commandment?*

*Answer: The sins forbidden by the tenth commandment are discontented restlessness with our lot in life, envy and depression when others succeed, along with all inappropriate and excessive desires for anything that belongs to someone else.*

The Westminster Larger Catechism, *1648*

**PRAYER**    O God, I have not produced a single righteous moment in my entire life. I have overrated my virtue and underestimated the depth and power of my sinfulness. I am deeply corrupt. O holy Christ, be all my righteousness! Cover all my sins with your merit. And then work your holiness deep down into the secret recesses of my soul, where I cannot put it, where no therapist can put it, where no drug can put it, but where it must penetrate if I am to be the holy person I ought to be, was made to be and long to be. In your holy name. Amen.

> *Lord, how secure my conscience was,*
> *And felt no inward dread.*
> *I was alive without thy law*
> *And thought my sins were dead.*
>
> *My hopes of heaven were firm and bright,*
> *But since the precept came,*
> *With a convincing power and light*
> *I find how vile I am.*
>
> *My guilt appeared but small before,*
> *Till terribly I saw*
> *How perfect, holy, just and pure*
> *Was thy eternal law!*
>
> *Then felt my soul the heavy load;*
> *My sins revived again.*
> *I had provoked a dreadful God,*
> *And all my hopes were slain.*
>
> *Thy gracious throne I bow beneath.*
> *Lord, thou alone canst save.*
> *O break the yoke of sin and death,*
> *And thus redeem the slave!*

*Isaac Watts, 1674–1748*

❖  ❖  ❖

So the law is good. But is a good thing still to blame for my living death? Unthinkable! It is *sin* that is to blame — the evil deep within me. But, for sin to be exposed as the damnable thing it really is, it took advantage of something good to produce death in me. Thanks to the commandment, sin was finally shown to be utterly, convincingly sinful. My eyes were opened to my true moral character. Theoretically, we all acknowledge that God's law is spiritual in nature and spiritually to be obeyed. But, unlike God's law, I am only natural. I am morally enfeebled. I live under the practical control of sin.—Romans 7:13-14

**PRAYER**   Holy Lord, you have confronted me. You have alerted me to my profound corruption within. In your law you gave me every incentive for obeying you. You gave me simple, clear instructions as to what you wanted from me. And I used that very law as a pretext for defying you. I do confess my sinfulness. I have neither mitigating excuse nor reforming power. I am sin's toy. It knows my points of weakness and plays with me at will. I therefore cling to your gospel promise with all my heart as my soul's only consolation. How long, O Lord, until I am freed from my condition, raised forever in the holy perfection of Christ? Until that longed-for moment, I will fix my faith on you alone, for my sinfulness cannot defeat your love. O sovereign Lord, show your redemptive power in me today, even amid my sinfulness. In the holy name of Christ. Amen.

> *Weak and irresolute is man.*
> *The purpose of today,*
> *Woven with pains into his plan,*
> *Tomorrow rends away.*

*The bow well bent and smart the spring,*
  *Vice seems already slain.*
*But passion rudely snaps the string,*
  *And it revives again.*

*Some foe to his upright intent*
  *Finds out his weaker part.*
*Virtue engages his assent,*
  *But pleasure wins his heart.*

*Bound on a voyage of awful length*
  *And dangers little known,*
*A stranger to superior strength,*
  *Man vainly trusts his own.*

*But oars can ne'er prevail*
  *To reach the distant coast.*
*The breath of heaven must swell the sail,*
  *Or all the toil is lost.*

*William Cowper, 1731–1800*

❖  ❖  ❖

The power of my sinfulness explains the conflict tearing
me apart. For I cannot understand my own behavior.
What I long for and admire I do not do, but the very
opposite. In fact, I do things I despise. So if I act against
my own better judgment, then I must agree—at least in
theory—that God's law is good. And because my conscience condemns my own sinful behavior, I can make
this distinction: In a sense, I am no longer the one gener-
ating all this evil. It is the sin within me that is produc-
ing it. This is no excuse. It only means that, even as I
condemn myself, I cannot help myself. I recognize that,
in myself, in the "me" that is merely natural, there is no

true virtue at all. Yes, my good intentions are constantly alert and responsive, always ready to volunteer. But the actual outcome in my behavior is another matter. I do not follow through with the good I want to do. Instead, what I actually do is the evil I do *not* want. Once again, if I end up doing what I do not want, then there is a sense in which it is no longer I doing it but this parasite sin living within me. So then, my experience reveals this principle governing my life: Even though I want to do what is good, evil keeps appearing in me. Although I joyfully affirm God's law in my deepest intentions, I observe another law active in my practical living. This other law fights against the law I approve of in theory, and my behavior is the casualty in the conflict. I have been taken captive by the law of sin, pervading and controlling my behavior. What a miserable man I am! Who will release me from this living death? Thanks be to God through Jesus Christ our Lord, who *will* set me free! But to sum up: I obey God's law in my good intentions, but in my old, fallen nature I still serve the law of sin.
—Romans 7:15-25

PRAYER    O Lord, your gospel is true to life. It reads me as much as I read it. How lofty, how grand, how noble are my intentions! But how ugly, how squalid, how embarrassing are my actions! I see your law for the holy thing it is. And I see myself, in my imagination, riding off on my white charger to do battle against sin. But so often, I am defeated and shamed and seen to be the fool I am. In this ongoing encounter between your law and my sinfulness, I am learning one simple truth: I really am a sinner, and I really hate it, and I really want you to be my Savior. Draw near to me now, dear Lord. Nurture within me an undying, persistent, rugged love for you that will fight on through the warfare of this life, never giving up and never giving in, but striving on for the holiness you have promised to perfect in me in heaven. Keep your bright promises before me, dear Lord, especially when I fall defeated in sin. In the holy name of Christ. Amen.

*I asked the Lord that I might grow*
   *In faith and love and every grace,*
*Might more of his salvation know*
   *And seek more earnestly his face.*

*'Twas he who taught me thus to pray*
   *And he, I trust, has answered prayer.*
*But it has been in such a way*
   *As almost drove me to despair.*

*I hoped that in some favored hour*
   *At once he'd answer my request,*
*And by his love's constraining power*
   *Subdue my sins and give me rest.*

*Instead of this, he made me feel*
   *The hidden evils of my heart,*
*And let the angry powers of hell*
   *Assault my soul in every part.*

*"Lord, why is this?" I trembling cried,*
   *"Wilt thou pursue thy worm to death?"*
*"'Tis in this way," the Lord replied,*
   *"I answer prayer for grace and faith."*

*"These inward trials I employ*
   *From self and pride to set thee free*
*And break thy schemes of earthly joy,*
   *That thou mayest seek thy all in me."*

*John Newton, 1725–1807*

# ROMANS

## CHAPTER 8

BUT WHY WILL FAITH succeed where law has failed? Because the life of faith is a life in the Spirit. By His Spirit, God will make us like Christ so that we truly obey his law, and nothing can defeat his loving purpose—Romans 8:1-39.

THE HOLY SPIRIT'S sanctifying presence within us is what sets us free from the power of sin—Romans 8:1-11

> So then, there is now no possibility that those who are united with Christ Jesus can be condemned to unrelieved misery here and eternal hell hereafter. For in Christ Jesus I am under a new arrangement for living, in which the Holy Spirit imparts life to me. This new order sets me free from the old arrangement for living, confined to sin and death. For what was impossible for the law all by itself, crippled as its power was due to our sinful nature, God accomplished. He sent his own Son in human form—except that Jesus was not sinful—to deal with our sin. Through his Son, God

doomed the power of our sin, so that the righteousness required by his law might be actualized in us, whose lives are not limited to our natural moral potential but give evidence of the Holy Spirit's sanctifying presence. —Romans 8:1-4

**PRAYER**     O Father, no possibility of my condemnation, and the certainty of the Spirit's sanctifying presence—how infinitely precious my gospel treasures are. The self-hatred and bewilderment of chapter seven will not be my experience forever. You have not only saved me from the penalty of my sin at the cross, but you have also undertaken to save me from the power of my sin through the Spirit. You give sanctification along with justification. I welcome both with an open heart. Come, Holy Spirit. Create new life in me now. Fill me now. Produce your sweet fruit in me now. Prove in me your power over sin and lead me into new paths of righteousness today. I long to walk in them. In the holy name of Christ. Amen.

> *I cannot speak of religion but I must lament that among so many pretenders to it so few understand what it means. Some place it in the understanding, in orthodox notions and opinions. . . . Others place it in the outward man, in a constant course of external duties and a model of performances. . . . Others again put all religion in the affections, in rapturous hearts and ecstatic devotion. . . . Thus are these things which have any resemblance of piety, and at the best are but means of obtaining it, or particular exercises of it, frequently mistaken for the whole of religion. . . . But certainly religion is quite another thing, and they who are acquainted with it will entertain far different thoughts and disdain all those shadows and false imitations of it. They know by experience that true religion is a union of the soul with God, a real*

*participation of the divine nature, the very image of*
*God drawn upon the soul, or, in the apostle's phrase,*
*it is "Christ formed within us." Briefly, I know not*
*how the nature of religion can be more fully expressed*
*than by calling it a divine life.*

*Henry Scougal, 1650–1678*

❖  ❖  ❖

Those who are limited to their own moral resources
regard their good intentions with confidence, but those
who have come under the Holy Spirit's control look to
the Spirit for his wisdom and power. The whole outlook
of natural morality breeds death, but the outlook and
orientation of the Spirit bears fruit in the richness and
fullness of life. The natural human outlook is fatal,
because its disobedient streak deep within is hostile to
God, the only source of true life. This hostility shows up
in a refusal to submit to God's law. In fact, one's self, all
by itself, is not even able to submit to God. So those who
are confined to their natural moral potential cannot
please God.—Romans 8:5-8

PRAYER    O Lord, you make a profound and searching distinction between natural human morality and authentic spirituality. A veneer of correctness would only conceal my
corruption within and utterly fail to touch the root of my sinfulness. Your gospel, O Lord, is not just another human religion. It is new and full of hope, because it replaces the best that
I can do with the best that you can do. Dear and blessed Savior,
I look up to you now with open-hearted faith and hope and
desire. Let me draw strength from you right now. Make me a
living example of authentic Christianity today, I pray. In the
holy name of Christ. Amen.

*March 26–27, 1951*

*Went on reading St Augustine. Interested to note that he left Carthage, where he had been teaching, to go to Rome because in Carthage his students were so undisciplined ("the license of the students is gross, and beyond all measure"). Convinced more than ever that St Augustine, and those like him, alone have found the answer to life, which is to "slaughter our self-conceits like birds, the curiosities by which we voyage through the secret ways of the abyss like the fish of the sea, our carnal lusts like the beasts of the field" in order that "you, O God, you the consuming fire, should burn up those dead cares and renew the men themselves to immortal life." Walking around St James's Park I thought intensely of the difference between Tolstoy and St Augustine. Tolstoy tried to achieve virtue, and particularly continence, through the exercise of his will; St Augustine saw that, for Man, there is no virtue without a miracle. Thus St Augustine's asceticism brought him serenity, and Tolstoy's anguish, conflict, and the final collapse of his life into tragic buffoonery.*

*Malcolm Muggeridge, 1903-1990*
*from his diary*

✧ ✧ ✧

But you have more going for you than your own high ideals. You now have the power of the Holy Spirit—on the assumption, of course, that God's Spirit does indeed live within you. (Anyone who does not possess the indwelling Spirit of Christ does not even belong to Christ.) And if Christ does live within you through his Spirit, then although your body is dying because of your sin, the Spirit will impart to you life eternal because of your justification. So if the Spirit of the One who raised

Jesus from the dead lives within you, he will eventually
make your mortal bodies alive with immortal life, as he
did with the risen Christ, through this same Spirit living
within you.—Romans 8:9-11

**PRAYER**   Lord above, although I still sin, I am now living
within a new framework. Your merit goes on compensating for
my guilt and your Spirit goes on conforming me to your image.
Though I am dying, I am destined to glorious immortality, by
your will and saving action. O Holy Spirit, nurture within me a
vivid sense of your presence with me and your claim upon me.
Make your power felt in my outlook on all of life. Mark me out
as one not limited to time but destined for eternity, not confined
to this world below but possessing a better world above. Let me
die to the claims of this kingdom and live in the sure and certain
hope of God's Kingdom. Set me apart to a life released from the
imperatives of this present evil age and in tune with the promise
of the age to come. Make me a true saint even as I remain, for
now, a sinner. In the holy name of Christ. Amen.

*Gracious Spirit, dwell with me!*
*I myself would gracious be.*
*And with words that help and heal*
*Would thy life in mine reveal.*
*And with actions bold and meek*
*Would for Christ, my Savior, speak.*

*Truthful Spirit, dwell with me!*
*I myself would truthful be.*
*And with wisdom kind and clear*
*Let thy life in mine appear,*
*And with actions brotherly*
*Speak my Lord's sincerity.*

*Mighty Spirit, dwell with me!*
*I myself would mighty be—*
*Mighty so as to prevail*
*Where unaided man must fail,*
*Ever by a mighty hope*
*Pressing on and bearing up.*

*Holy Spirit, dwell with me!*
*I myself would holy be.*
*Separate from sin, I would*
*Choose and cherish all things good.*
*And whatever I can be*
*Give to him who gave me thee.*

*Thomas T. Lynch, 1818–1871*

❖   ❖   ❖

OUR PART IN our sanctification is, by the power of the Spirit, to mortify our sins—Romans 8:12-14

So then, dear friends, we owe nothing to our old sinful nature with its futile attempts at self-perfection. If you draw on nothing more than your own native moral capacities, you will surely die. But if you put to death your sinful impulses by the power of the Spirit, you will live. For all who are moved along by the Spirit of God in this new direction—toward the divinely-enabled disciplines of holiness—are the true children of God.
—Romans 8:12-14

PRAYER    Father in heaven, I want to learn what it means to mortify the deeds of the flesh by the power of the Spirit. I want to *live*. I want to live *as a child of God*. I want Spirit-empowered destruction of sin, along with new holiness of life, in deep personal communion with you. Blessed Holy Spirit, lead me

along, step by step, into these experiences, whatever it takes.
Lead this generation of your church there as well, O Lord, for
we are being overwhelmed with a tidal wave of sin here in the
modern world. Spirit-given holiness, Lord—flood your church
with a renewal of Spirit-given holiness today. In the holy name
of Christ. Amen.

> *Suppose someone earnestly desires to mortify sin. He
> prays, sighs, groans and longs for deliverance.
> Meanwhile, he neglects his devotional reading, his
> prayer life, his meditations with God. Then he won-
> ders why sin retains its power in his life. This is a
> common condition among men. The Israelites, under
> a sense of sin, drew near to God with much diligence
> and earnestness in prayer and fasting. "They seek me
> daily and delight to know my ways . . . they ask of me
> the ordinances of justice; they take delight in
> approaching God" (Isaiah 58:2). Yet God rejected it
> all. Their fastings could not heal them because, while
> they were particular in that duty, they were careless
> about others. The Israelites had an ulcerous wound
> they could never heal themselves, for they never hated
> sin as sin. Their blindness proceeded from self-love.
> Without obedience to all of God's Word and all of
> God's provisions for salvation, isolated acts of morti-
> fication avail little. . . . Hating one particular sin or
> weakness is not enough; we must have a general dis-
> position of life before God. The outbreak of one par-
> ticular sin may only be symptomatic of a general
> condition of sickness, for sin lies at the root of our
> being. Thus God allows one sin to perplex us and
> gain strength over us, in order to chasten us and
> allow us to see our lukewarmness before the Lord.
> Indeed, the rage and dominance of a particular lust or
> sin in us commonly results from a careless, negligent
> course of life. . . . We cannot resist God's chastening if*

*we desire to mortify sin. We only obtain mortification
of sin in one area of life as we remain open to the
need of mortification in every area.*

*John Owen, 1616–1683*

✧   ✧   ✧

THE INDWELLING HOLY SPIRIT bonds us to God with childlike
affection—Romans 8:15-17

> The Spirit has not made you slaves, so that you must for-
> ever cringe in dread of God every time you fail. No, not
> anymore! The Spirit has now made us God's children, so
> that we cry out to him, "Father! Father!" It is God's own
> Spirit prompting us in this way, assuring us with deep affec-
> tions that we really are children of God. And since we are
> God's children, we stand to inherit all of God's promises in
> the gospel. We are heirs of God, then, and fellow-heirs with
> Christ—as long as we share his sufferings now so that we
> may also share his glory then.—Romans 8:15-17

PRAYER    Father, Father, I find deep within my heart a persistent longing for you. As much as I violate it, that longing
does not die. It wanes. It fluctuates. But it does not die, for
you have put it there and you sustain it by your grace. You
have laid claim to my love, and you will not be denied. And
this is how I know that I really am your child—amid all my
failure, my soul keeps gravitating toward you. You know all
things, Lord. You know how often I deny you. But you also
know that I truly love you. And now I know that my yearning will not be frustrated but will be infinitely, richly, glori-
ously fulfilled when this life is finally over. I will enter into my
heavenly inheritance and see you face to face. Your bright
presence will be worth it all, blessed God above. In the holy
name of Christ. Amen.

*Thyself, O my God, thyself for thine own sake, above
all things else I love. Thyself I desire. Thyself as my last
end I long for. Thyself for thine own sake, not aught
else whatsoever, alway and in all things I seek with all
my heart and marrow, with groaning and weeping,
with unbroken toil and grief. What wilt thou render me
therefore for my last end? If thou render me not thyself, thou renderest nought. If thou give me not thyself,
thou givest nought. If I find not thyself, I find nought.
To no purpose thou rewardest me but dost wring me
sore. For, or ever I sought thee, I hoped to find thee at
the last and to keep thee. And with this honied hope in
all my toils was I sweetly comforted. But now, if thou
have denied me thyself, what else soever thou give me,
frustrate of so high an hope, and that not for a little
space but forever, shall I not alway languish with love,
mourn with languishing, grieve with mourning, bewail
with grief, and weep for that alway I shall abide empty
and void? Shall I not sorrow inconsolably, complain
unceasingly, be wrung unendingly? This is not thy
property, O best, most gracious, most loving God. In
no wise is it congruous, no wise it sorteth. Make me
therefore, O best my God, in the life present alway to
love thyself for thyself before all things, to seek thee in
all things, and at the last in the life to come to find and
to keep thee forever.*

*Lancelot Andrewes, 1555–1626*

✧   ✧   ✧

OUR PRESENT SUFFERING is leading us to our future glory, by the
will of God—Romans 8:18-30

But there is no one-for-one correspondence between
our present suffering and our future glory. As I calcu-

late it, the hardships that make this present age what it
is are *nothing* compared with the glory soon to be
revealed to us. This is why the natural creation waits in
hushed suspense, with an aching longing, for the children of God finally to be revealed for what they truly
are. After all, nature itself shares in the present sorrows.
Its true potential has been frustrated by a pervasive
futility, against its own inclination and design, by God's
curse. But there is hope, for even the creation will be
liberated from its bondage to decay when it enters into
the freedom of the glory promised to God's children.
—Romans 8:18-21

**PRAYER**    O Father, a new heavens, a new earth, a new
humanity—how wide is the scope of your gospel! It does not
offer me a private religious preference. It leads me into the
secrets of the universe. I affirm your plan for all things. I submit myself to your will for my particular life, including the
hardships you have ordained for me. Lead me into the brilliant
glory just ahead, where my tears will be wiped away forever,
where the sorrows of this life will be only a fading memory,
swallowed up in a heavenly ocean of pure delight. O God, I
long to be lifted up out of time, out of this present age, out of
my sins, to be with you forever. Keep my heart ablaze for you,
dear Lord, until you take me home. In the holy name of
Christ. Amen.

> *My rest is in heaven; my rest is not here.*
> *Then why should I murmur when trials*
> *are near?*
> *Be hushed, my dark spirit! The worst that*
> *can come*
> *But shortens thy journey and hastens*
> *thee home.*

*It is not for me to be seeking my bliss*
*And building my hopes in a region like this.*
*I look for a city which hands have not piled,*
*I pant for a country by sin undefiled.*

*Let doubt then and danger my progress oppose;*
*They only make heaven more sweet at the*
*close.*
*Come joy or come sorrow, whate'er may befall,*
*An hour with my God will make up for it all.*

*Henry Francis Lyte, 1793–1847*

❖  ❖  ❖

We know that all of nature together groans in agony and writhes in birth-pains right up to the present moment. And not only nature, but we ourselves, who already manifest the initial evidences of the Spirit's indwelling life—even we groan in agony as we await the full experience of our adoption as God's children, the transformation of our bodies. For we have not yet seen the whole of our salvation. We still look forward to it as our future hope. Hope, by definition, does not yet have what it hopes for. After all, who "hopes" for a present possession? But if we have set our hope on something we do not yet experience, we must look forward to it with patient endurance.—Romans 8:22-25

PRAYER    Lord in heaven, you never intended that this earthly life would be a Final Experience. You mean it to be a transitional phase on my way to the Final Experience, when I will see your face, when I will be fully cleansed of sin, when my body will be raised immortal and all the sorrows of this life will be over forever. But not yet. It is coming. It is certain. But it is not here yet. O Father, keep me faithful to this glorious vision of what will be.

Do not allow me to be seduced by the degrading idols and distractions of this age. Never let me stoop to a life of licking the earth, when I am destined for heaven. Keep me alert to my hope, and lead me all the way to my true home with you above, I pray. In the holy name of Christ. Amen.

> I pray, O God, that I may know you, that I may love you, so that I may rejoice in you. And if I cannot do this to the full in this life, at least let me go forward from day to day until that joy comes to fullness. Let the knowledge of you go forward in me here, and there let it be made full. Let love for you increase, and there let it be full, so that here my joy may be great in hope and there it may be full in reality. O Lord, through your Son, you command us—rather, you counsel us— to ask, and you promise that we shall receive, that our joy may be full. O Lord, I ask what you counsel through our wonderful Counselor. Let me receive what you promise through your truth, that my joy may be full. Meanwhile, let my mind meditate upon it, let my tongue speak of it. Let my heart love it, let my tongue discourse upon it. Let my soul hunger for it, let my flesh thirst for it, let my whole being desire it, until I enter into the joy of my Lord, who is the triune and one God, blessed forever. Amen.
>
> Anselm, ca. 1033–1109

❖  ❖  ❖

And the Holy Spirit also helps us in our weak attempts to pray. In the bewilderment of this life we sometimes do not know what we ought to be asking for. But the Spirit himself pleads for us in our inarticulate groanings. And God, who searches our hearts, understands what the Spirit means, because he pleads for God's people in perfect accord with the Father's own will. Moreover, we know that all the events of our lives are orchestrated by God's sovereign will for our ultimate good, the salvation which belongs to all who love God, to all who have been called in his plan. That plan began in eternity past, carries on into eternity future and guarantees our full salvation. For all whom God chose long ago, the same ones he also predestined to become perfect images of his Son, so that the Son would be first in rank within a huge family. And all whom God predestined, the same ones he also called to faith. And all whom he called to faith, the same ones he also justified. And all whom he justified, the same ones he has also begun to glorify. No one is lost along the way.—Romans 8:26-30

**PRAYER**    O Father, your love has provided everything. I did not even initiate our relationship with an appeal of faith. My faith entered the picture only long after you had set everything in motion. You marked me with your love before time began. You provided a Savior for me long ago. You sent your Spirit to me, prompting the movements of faith within my dead heart. It is all of grace, all of love, all of you. Father, I give my life back to you. I surrender to the pilgrimage you have ordained for me, including the hardships. Have your way with me, O God of love, as you lead me on to eternal glory. In the holy name of Christ. Amen.

> *God moves in a mysterious way*
> *His wonders to perform.*
> *He plants his footsteps in the sea,*
> *And rides upon the storm.*
>
> *Deep in unfathomable mines*
> *Of never-failing skill,*
> *He treasures up his bright designs*
> *And works his sovereign will.*

*Ye fearful saints, fresh courage take.*
*The clouds ye so much dread*
*Are big with mercy, and shall break*
*In blessings on your head.*

*Judge not the Lord by feeble sense,*
*But trust him for his grace.*
*Behind a frowning providence*
*He hides a smiling face.*

*His purposes will ripen fast,*
*Unfolding every hour.*
*The bud may have a bitter taste,*
*But sweet will be the flower.*

*Blind unbelief is sure to err,*
*And scan his work in vain.*
*God is his own interpreter,*
*And he will make it plain.*

*William Cowper, 1773*
*shortly before his second*
*attack of insanity*

❖ ❖ ❖

WE ARE FOREVER SAFE, for God's saving love will never let us go
—Romans 8:31-39

What lesson then should we take from all of this? One
thing. If God is on our side, who can deprive us of our full
salvation? If God did not even spare his own Son but gave
him up at the cross for us all, how could he possibly withhold anything else? Won't he give us everything we need
for salvation? Who could mount an effective attack
against the very people whom God has already chosen to

be on his side? God is himself the one who clears us of all our guilt by the merit of Christ. So who could argue against that defense? We have no one less than Christ Jesus, who died, who was also raised and who is now positioned at God's right hand where he pleads for us. So what would have to happen to cut us off from the saving love of Christ? Affliction? Anguish? Persecution? Starvation? Exposure? Danger? Execution? The Scriptures acknowledge that these terrible things do happen to God's people:

*For your sake we are put to death all day long,*
*we are treated like sheep ready for slaughter.*

But in all our sufferings we achieve total victory through Christ who loved us, for he will not let our faith die. It keeps springing back, overcoming whatever adversities we encounter.—Romans 8:31-37

**PRAYER**    O triumphant Man of Sorrows, why am I so afraid of suffering? Have I forgotten that you draw near to your sufferers with special manifestations of your mercies, more than compensating for the adversity? Have I forgotten that you convict the world through a suffering, not a triumphant, church? Have I forgotten that it is not by might, nor by power, but by your Spirit? That when I am weak I am strong? That your grace is made perfect in my weakness? That the willing loss of earthly things for the sake of heavenly things is a powerful witness to the reality of those unseen treasures before a world enslaved to the tangible? Lord, I am no hero. I only want to live a quiet life with my family and be left alone to get on with my ministry. But the world is becoming increasingly hostile to your claims. And I am learning that, if you do ordain that I should seal my testimony to you with suffering, I have nothing to fear. You will be there for me. You will be there at my side. You will not let my faith die and discredit you. Nothing can wrench me out of your loving embrace. I now receive, and I treasure, your assurance and peace. In your holy name. Amen.

*Be not afraid at His sweet, lovely and desirable cross, for
although I have not been able because of my wounds to
lift up or lay down my head but as I was helped, yet I
was never in better case all my life. . . . He has so won-
derfully shined on me with the sense of His redeeming,
strengthening, assisting, supporting, through-bearing,
pardoning and reconciling love, grace and mercy, that my
soul doth long to be freed of bodily infirmities and
earthly organs, so that I may flee to His Royal Palace,
even the Heavenly Habitation of my God, where I am
sure of a crown put on my head and a palm put in my
hand and a new song in my mouth, even the song of
Moses and of the Lamb, so that I may bless, praise, magnify and extol Him for what He hath done to me and for
me. Wherefore I bid farewell to all my dear fellow-suffer-
ers for the testimony of Jesus, who are wandering in dens
and caves. Farewell, my children; study holiness in all
your ways, and praise the Lord for what He hath done
for me, and tell all my Christian friends to praise Him on
my account. Farewell, sweet Bible, and wanderings and
contendings for truth. Welcome, death. Welcome, the
City of my God where I shall see Him and be enabled to
serve Him eternally with full freedom. Welcome, blessed
company, the angels and spirits of just men made perfect.
But above all, welcome, welcome, welcome, our glorious
and alone God, Father, Son and Holy Ghost. Into Thy
hands I commit my spirit, for Thou art worthy. Amen.*

*"Last and Dying Testimony" of John Nisbet, 1685
Scottish Covenanter and martyr
written in prison shortly before his hanging*

❖   ❖   ❖

In fact, I am convinced that nothing can rob us of our salvation—neither the terrors of death nor the enticements of
life, neither angels nor demons, neither present-day troubles

nor future crises, nor cosmic powers, nor anything in heaven above nor anything in hell below, indeed, *nothing* in the entire created order will be able to separate us from the saving love of God in Christ Jesus our Lord.—Romans 8:38-39

**PRAYER**    Almighty God and and merciful Father, infinite in grace and sovereign in majesty, that you would trouble yourself to provide so fully for me, to ensure that my joy in Christ would not, could not, be jeopardized by anything at all, however evil or bizarre, that you would care that much to design my salvation so securely and infallibly, that you would pay so much in the Son to get so little in  me, and that you would not only do so but also *tell* me that you have done so, enabling me to enjoy the security of your unchanging love—I bow low before you in wonder. It is all by your grace and all to your glory. I worship you now, blessed God. I will worship you forever. In the holy name of Christ. Amen.

*From the depths of hell I call the fiends, and from this earth I call the tried and afflicted believers, and to heaven I appeal, and challenge the long experience of the blood-washed host, and there is not to be found in the three realms a single person who can bear witness to one fact which can disprove the faithfulness of God or weaken his claim to be trusted by his servants. There are many things that may or may not happen, but this I know shall happen—*

> *He shall present my soul*
> *Unblemished and complete*
> *Before the glory of his face*
> *With joys divinely great.*

*All the purposes of man have been defeated, but not the purposes of God. He is a promise-keeping God, and every one of his people shall prove it to be so.*

*Charles Haddon Spurgeon, 1834–1892*

# ROMANS

## CHAPTER 9

BUT CAN WE REALLY TRUST God never to abandon us, since it appears that he has abandoned his ancient people Israel? Can we count on God's promises to be utterly sure? Yes, when we consider the ways of God—Romans 9:1-11:36

THE HEART-RENDING PARADOX is that Israel, so far from God, is nevertheless rich with divine privilege—Romans 9:1-5

But if nothing can separate us from God's love, what about Israel? If God's loving purpose for *them* has failed, couldn't his loving purpose for *us* fail as well? Now let me bare my heart. (Before Christ my Judge, I am telling the plain truth. I am not faking anything, as my untroubled conscience under the scrutiny of the Holy Spirit confirms within me.) Profound is my grief! Constant is my anguish! I would pray—if it were permissible—that my own soul be damned, if that would save my brothers, my people by natural descent, the Israelites. They are so near to God, and yet so far from him. Think of their privileges:

*Their adoption by God as his chosen nation,*
*the glory of God made manifest in their sight,*
*their covenant engagements to God;*
*the knowledge of truth and right through God's law,*
*the divinely authorized liturgy offering God's*
*acceptance,*
*the promises from God of great things still*
*in store.*

Israel can claim the patriarchs—Abraham, Isaac, Jacob. Indeed, from Israel, in terms of natural descent, came the very Christ himself, who is supreme over all as God blessed forever. Amen.—Romans 9:1-5

**PRAYER**    O Lord God, what privileges you have showered upon me as well. You have joined me to Christ and to his Body, the church, by your Spirit. You have put into my hands your holy Word, with its great and precious promises. You have marked me as your own through baptism. You draw near to me in fellowship at your table. And great privilege incurs great responsibility. O God, do not let me squander my treasures. Let me be a wise steward of your gifts, translating rich opportunity into even richer possession. Add this one privilege on top of all the others, dear Lord—that I would be as responsive as I am favored. In the holy name of Christ, who is supreme over all as God blessed forever, most worthy of my complete devotion. Amen.

*I saw that there was a way to Hell even from the*
*Gates of Heaven, as well as from the City of*
*Destruction.*

> *John Bunyan,*
> The Pilgrim's Progress, *1688*

❖ ❖ ❖

BUT GOD NEVER PROMISED the salvation of every single descendant of Abraham. He himself decides who will be a true Israelite—Romans 9:6-13

> So what are we to make of Israel, so favored and yet so poor? Has their unbelief frustrated God's purpose? Has God tried, but failed? It is *not* as though God's intentions have failed to materialize, for not all of Israel is the true Israel. While all of them are outwardly privileged, you see, not all of them are inwardly authentic. Neither are all the physical descendants of Abraham God's special people. But, as God said to him, "Your true successors will be identified through the line of Isaac, your son by Sarah, not through Ishmael, your son by Hagar." In other words, the true Israel of God is to be defined not as the physical descendants of Abraham *per se* but as those who are born through the power of God's infallible promise. For how was Isaac born? God made a promise: "At the appointed time I will visit you with the fulfillment of my word, and Sarah will bear a son."
> —Romans 9:6-9

PRAYER O Lord God, you make distinctions between people—deeply searching distinctions. You know all who are truly your own and all who are not. And all whom you have chosen you bless with true spiritual life within. O God, create new life today, I pray, amid the deadness pervading the human race, according to your sovereign will. Hover over this world, Creator Savior. Say again, "Let there be light." Command new growth and color and vibrancy where now there is only deadness. Impart true life where now there is only religion. Grant spirituality where now there is mere enthusiasm. We cannot renew ourselves, but you can renew us. You need only speak the word, and it is done. O blessed God, spread your mercies widely in the world today. And as you do, remember *my* family. Remember *my* church and *my* community. Even though we sin against you, do not deal with us judicially but mercifully, O sovereign God. In the holy name of Christ. Amen.

> *Be careful how you treat God, my friends. You may say to yourself, "I can sin against God, and then, of course, I can repent and go back and find God whenever I want him." You try it. And you will sometimes find that not only can you not find God but that you do not even want to. You will be aware of a terrible hardness, a callosity in your heart. And you can do nothing about it. And then you suddenly realize that it is God punishing you in order to reveal your sinfulness and your vileness to you. And there is only one thing to do. You turn back to him and you say, "Oh God, do not go on dealing with me judicially, though I deserve it. Soften my heart. Melt me. I cannot do it myself." You cast yourself utterly upon his mercy and upon his compassion.*
>
> *Martyn Lloyd-Jones, 1899–1981*

❖   ❖   ❖

And not only that. The fact that God selects his own was made even clearer in the next generation. Rebecca became pregnant by Isaac our forefather. From one mother, one father, and one act of intercourse, came twin sons, Esau and Jacob. But before they were even born, before they had a chance to do anything good or bad as if to influence the outcome, God chose Jacob. God decides for himself who his people will be. And so that his purpose (which works out in history according to a distinguishing pattern of selection) would be established in all its sovereign character, independent of human merits and determined only by God who calls whomever he wills, it was said to Rebecca, "Your older son Esau will serve your younger son Jacob." This is explained by yet another Old Testament declaration: "Jacob I have favored, but Esau I have excluded."—Romans 9:10-13

**PRAYER** O God, I did not decide whether I would be favored or excluded. You did. Behind, within and around my choice of you was your prior choice of me. All rights are yours. All entitlements are yours. All power is yours. I exist for you. I exist by you. I exist under you. O awesome God, I stand only by your mercy. With Moses, I make haste to bow low in worship. I abase myself before you. I yield to you. I despise myself, compared with you. I am not the center of reality with you as my servant, but you are the center of reality and I am your servant. O sovereign Master, O Most High, I rest in your sovereign decree of love, which makes me as secure in Christ as I am helpless in myself. In his holy name. Amen.

> *Keep silence, all created things,*
> *And wait your Maker's nod;*
> *My soul stands trembling while she sings*
> *The honors of her God.*

> *Life, death and hell and worlds unknown*
> *Hang on his firm decree;*
> *He sits on no precarious throne,*
> *Nor borrows leave to be.*

> *Chained to his throne a volume lies,*
> *With all the fates of men,*
> *With every angel's form and size*
> *Drawn by the eternal pen.*

*His providence unfolds the book*
*And makes his counsels shine;*
*Each opening leaf and every stroke*
*Fulfills some deep design.*

*In thy fair book of life and grace,*
*O may I find my name*
*Recorded in some humble place,*
*Beneath my Lord the Lamb.*

                                    Isaac Watts, 1674–1748


                          ✧   ✧   ✧


AND GOD IS NOT WRONG to choose whomever he wills, because in exercising his sovereign freedom he is displaying his own glorious nature—Romans 9:14-18

So God never intended every single descendant of Abraham to be included in the true Israel. But then, is that *fair*? Is it wrong of God to distinguish between people before they even have a chance? There is no injustice in God, is there? Unthinkable! He said to Moses, "I reserve the right to show mercy to whomever I choose and to shower compassion upon whomever I choose. It is entirely up to me, and my freedom demonstrates my glory." In other words, God is always just, because he is always true to himself. So then, being included in God's chosen people is not a matter of human resolve or commitment; it is up to God who shows mercy. God magnified himself again when he said to Pharaoh, "For this very reason I brought you into existence and exalted you to prominence—so that I might display through you my power and so that my glorious name might be broadcast far and wide." So then, God is the one to decide whom he will favor with mercy, and God is the one to decide whom he will exclude with a hard heart. And my point is that God is *right* to put his glory on display by exercising his prerogatives as God.—Romans 9:14-18

PRAYER    Most High God, I take my shoes off my feet, for I am standing on holy ground. I humbly acknowledge that you are *right* not to un-god yourself. You are *right* not to subordinate yourself to defiant human demands. You are *right* to exalt your supremacy over all things. You are God; I am not. I am the clay; you are the Potter. You have the rightful power to make of me whatever you please. And yet to me, even me, you have been pleased to display the glory of your mercy in Christ. Let me, O Lord, like the contrite whore, weep with joy and kiss your feet. In the holy name of Christ. Amen.

> *There has been a wonderful alteration in my mind with respect to the doctrine of God's sovereignty. . . . The doctrine has very often appeared exceedingly pleasant, bright and sweet. Absolute sovereignty is what I love to ascribe to God.*
>
> Jonathan Edwards, 1703–1758

❖ ❖ ❖

NEITHER IS GOD WRONG to judge sinners, because the full display of his glorious nature entails a demonstration of both wrath and (much closer to his heart) mercy—Romans 9:19-23

But if our spiritual condition is determined ultimately by God's will, I know what you will say next. You will demand of God, "Why do you still hold me responsible? How can you judge *me* for a situation *you* control? After all, who has ever hindered the fulfillment of your sovereign purpose? So if you find me guilty, God, you are a hypocrite!" *Quite the contrary!* How do you, mere man, have the gall to challenge God? The very tone of your question reveals your insolence. Think about it. Does a statue say to its sculptor, "Why did you make me like this? I object!" Who has the right to guide the chisel? Or think of a potter. Is he not entitled to take his lump of clay and make one part of it into a lovely vase and another part into a common pot?—Romans 9:19-21

**PRAYER**    O Most High God, I frankly confess that there is in me, no less than in the veriest scoffer, a quick readiness to find fault with you. Dark, dark thoughts of you cloud my mind and impair my judgment. I magnify my own capacity for moral wisdom and minimize yours. I would make you my victim by claiming that I am your victim. In effect, I insist that you limit yourself to accommodate me. I demand that you withhold the full expression of your glorious nature so that I can have my own way here in the Kingdom of Self. O holy God, I am like a beast before you. Underneath my grand posturing is a profound hatred of you, along with a desperate resolve to find an excuse, *any* excuse, for the guilt troubling my conscience. O bright and blessed God above, you are not the hypocrite; I am. Forgive my arrogant presumption, as if *I* could look down in judgment upon *you.* Come and tame my ego. Come and teach me shame. In the holy name of Christ. Amen.

*As long as a man is thinking of God as an examiner*
*who has set him a sort of paper to do or as the oppo-*
*site party in a sort of bargain—as long as he is thinking*
*of claims and counterclaims between himself and*
*God—he is not yet in the right relation to Him. He is*
*misunderstanding what he is and what God is.*

C. S. Lewis, 1898–1963

❖  ❖  ❖

And what if God, because he wanted to demonstrate his wrath and show his power—what if he tolerated with great restraint, until they were ripe for judgment, those "earthenware vessels" destined for wrath and prepared for destruction? Does not God have the right to do this? Or will we demand that God reveal only that part of his nature agreeable with our own preferences? And what if God wanted to put on even grander display the infinite treasure-store of his glorious nature by lavishing mercy upon others, who in themselves were also mere "earthenware vessels" but whom he had predestined to glory? Does not God have the right to do that as well? Does not God have the right to reveal the full range of his sublime character by lifting high his mercy against the backdrop of his wrath? Is not God right to be fully God? —Romans 9:22-23

**PRAYER**    O Lord, God of wrath, God of mercy, you are the sovereign Determiner of every human life. You are rightful Judge; you are merciful Savior. How vast is your glory. You are a God complex enough, profound enough, paradoxical enough, that we will never exhaust you. We will never discover that, after all, you are really just like us, only bigger. You are, in truth, in another category altogether. You are *God*. I bow low before you, O my merciful God, for you have laid your finger tenderly upon my forehead and marked me out for glory—*me*, a mere earthen vessel. Eternity in your bright presence cannot come soon enough. In the holy name of Christ. Amen.

*There is no attribute of God more comforting to His children than the doctrine of Divine Sovereignty. Under the most adverse conditions, in the most severe troubles, they believe that Sovereignty hath ordained their afflictions, that Sovereignty overrules them, and that Sovereignty will sanctify them all. There is nothing for which the children of God ought more earnestly to contend than the dominion of their Master over all creation—the kingship of God over all the works of His own hands—the throne of God, and His right to sit upon that throne. On the other hand, there is no doctrine more hated by worldlings, no truth of which they have made such a football, as the great, stupendous, but yet most certain doctrine of the Sovereignty of the infinite Jehovah. Men will allow God to be everywhere except upon His throne. They will allow Him to be in His workshop to fashion worlds and to make stars. They will allow Him to be in His almonry to dispense His alms and bestow His bounties. They will allow Him to sustain the earth and bear up the pillars thereof, or light the lamps of heaven, or rule the waves of the ever-moving ocean. But when God ascends His throne, His creatures then gnash their teeth. And when we proclaim an enthroned God, and His right to do as He wills with His own, to dispose of His creatures as He thinks well, without consulting them in the matter, then it is at that we are hissed and execrated, and then it is that men turn a deaf ear to us, for God on His throne is not the God they love. They love Him anywhere better than they do when He sits with His sceptre in His hand and His crown upon His head. But it is God upon the throne that we love to preach. It is God upon His throne whom we trust. It is God upon His throne of whom we speak.*

Charles Haddon Spurgeon, 1834-1892

❖ ❖ ❖

THE OLD TESTAMENT itself confirms God's way of selecting his own, namely, that the true Israel includes not all the Jews but it does include both Jews and Gentiles—Romans 9:24-29

> And we believers in Christ are the divine Potter's vessels of mercy. He has called us not only from the Jews but also from the Gentiles, as it says in the prophecy of Hosea,
>
> > *I will call those who are not my people into*
> > *    existence as my people,*
> > *and those who have been unloved I will love.*
> > *And in the very condition which warranted*
> > *    that they be told, "You are not my people,"*
> > *even there I will call them to become children*
> > *    of the living God.*
>
> But Isaiah lifts up a prophetic cry concerning ethnic Israel: "The number of the children of Israel could equal the grains of sand on the seashore, but still only the remnant will be saved. For the Lord will fulfill his sovereign decree in this world, accomplishing it completely and decisively." This is in line with what Isaiah had written earlier:
>
> > *If the Lord of Hosts had not mercifully left us*
> > *    a few survivors,*
> > *we would have been consumed like Sodom,*
> > *we would have been wiped out like Gomorrah.*
>
> But, mercifully, the chosen remnant of Israel continues in Christ.—Romans 9:24-29

**PRAYER**    Merciful Lord, you will not allow our sins to defeat your purpose. You stretch out your hand to reverse our Gadarene rush after the idols. You turn us around and lead us in a new direction. You pour your love out upon us even though we deserve your wrath. You will make us true children of the living God. And all this mercy is the overflow of your glory, which you are putting on display before the whole universe. Truly, your goodness is of a spreading nature! I open my heart now to receive your mercy as my dearest treasure and your greatest glory. In the holy name of Christ. Amen.

> *On wings of love the Savior flies,*
>     *And freely left his native skies to take a*
>     *human birth.*
> *The wise and righteous men go near,*
>     *His wonders see, his sermons hear, and think*
>     *him nothing worth.*
>
> *A remnant small of humble souls*
>     *His grace mysteriously controls by sweet*
>     *alluring call.*
> *They hear it, and his person view,*
>     *They learn to love, and follow too, and take*
>     *him for their all.*
>
> *One of the remnant I would be,*
>     *A soul devoted unto thee, allured by thy voice;*
> *No more on gaudy idols gaze,*
>     *No longer tinsel grandeur praise, but fix on*
>     *thee my choice.*
>
>                                  *John Berridge, 1716–1793*

❖ ❖ ❖

SO WHAT HAS GONE WRONG with Israel, and how did Gentiles find their way into the true Israel? The answer lies in the offense of the gospel—Christ himself—Romans 9:30-10:4

**What then shall we conclude? That Gentiles, who typically do not even pursue justification, have laid hold of it—justification by faith, that is. But Israel, so ardently pursuing the very law which points the way to justification, has not arrived at the goal intended by the law.**

For what reason? Because their whole approach has been misguided. They have tried to reach the goal not by the humility of faith but by their own meritorious achievements. In the course of their pursuit they have tripped over a stone, Christ himself, put in the pathway to catch all self-trusting seekers. As it is written,

> I am putting in Zion a Stone which will make
> people stumble and a Rock which will make them fall;
> but the one who grounds his faith on this firm
> Foundation will not regret it on the great day of
> judgment.

—Romans 9:30-33

**PRAYER**   O Lord God, here, out in front of the shadow concealing the mystery of your sovereignty, you have placed in clearer view, obscured by nothing but the darkness of human sin, the more observable reason why only a remnant of Israel is saved. And that reason is the necessity of personal submission to your ways, to your path, to your Christ. O Jesus, I am an inconstant seeker, but you are a great Savior. I submit to you. I trust in you. I rest on you, my only firm Foundation. Let me remain true to this faith throughout my life, no matter what the cost. Then, when my eyes close in death, when I rise to stand before your judgment throne, I will have no regrets. In your holy name. Amen.

> Let us often read again the simple, strong assurance
> which closes this chapter of mysteries: "He who confides
> in Him shall not be put to shame." . . . From that safe
> Place no hurried retreat shall ever need to be beaten.
> That Fortress cannot be stormed. It cannot be surprised.
> It cannot crumble. For "It is He," the Son, the Lamb of
> God, the sinner's everlasting Righteousness, the believer's
> unfailing Source of peace, of purity and of power.
>
> Handley C. G. Moule, 1841–1920

# ROMANS

## CHAPTER 10

Dear friends, my heart's longing and my plea to God for my people, the Jews, are that they would be saved. Let me go on record and vouch for their sincerity. They are passionately devoted to God! But they fail to grasp what God really wants from them. Misunderstanding God's way of justification, and in their self-assurance trying to establish their own hard-won justification, they have not submitted to the humbling, the brokenness, the self-emptying entailed in God's method of justification. They do not accept that *Christ* is the true meaning and ultimate goal of the law. All its commands, promises and rituals whisper *Christ*. The law, correctly understood, leads us to *Christ* as the decisive end to all legalistic self-improvement, for he gives the gift of justification to everyone who *believes.*—Romans 10:1-4

**PRAYER**    O Lord God, I acknowledge that zeal for you, precisely because it feels so right, can deceive, concealing my actual need for you at a level of my being deeper than my own fervor can reach. O Lord, let me know the reality of myself and the fullness of Christ. Let me be stripped, that I may be clothed. Let me be wounded, that I may be healed. Let me be shamed, that I may be glorified in Christ, my all-sufficient Savior. Whatever I must lose, let me gain Christ and be found complete in him alone. In his holy name. Amen.

*Jesus Christ came to blind those who saw clearly, and to give sight to the blind; to heal the sick, and leave the healthy to die; to call to repentance and to justify sinners, and to leave the righteous in their sins; to fill the needy, and leave the rich empty.*

*Blaise Pascal, 1623-1662*

*The one true goal or resting-place where doubt and weariness, the stings of a pricking conscience and the longings of an unsatisfied soul would all be quieted is Christ himself. Not the church, but Christ. Not doctrine, but Christ. Not forms, but Christ. Not ceremonies, but Christ. Christ, the God-man, giving his life for ours, sealing the everlasting covenant and making peace for us through the blood of his cross. Christ the divine storehouse of all light and truth, "in whom are hid all the treasures of wisdom and knowledge" (Colossians 2:3). Christ the infinite vessel, filled with the Holy Spirit, the Enlightener, the Teacher, the Comforter, so that "of his fullness we have all received, and grace upon grace" (John 1:16). This, this alone, is the vexed souls's refuge, its rock to build on, its home to abide in, till the great tempter be bound and every conflict ended in victory.*

*Horatius Bonar, 1808-1889*

❖ ❖ ❖

ISRAEL'S REJECTION OF Christ and of justification by faith is sadly
ironic and morally blameworthy, for the very law they cling to
points beyond itself to Christ and the way of faith
—Romans 10:5-13

> Our justification must be all of Christ, for Moses him-
> self, the great lawgiver, writes of the hopeless quest of
> justification by law: "Only the one who fulfills the law's
> demands will win true life." But justification by faith
> also has something to say. It warns us, in the words of
> the law itself, not to deny what God has graciously pro-
> vided for us:
>
> > *Never create imaginary problems which make*
> > *justification seem totally out of reach. For exam-*
> > *ple, don't say things like, "Who could possibly*
> > *ascend into heaven to bring Christ down?," as if*
> > *he had not come down to us already! Or, "Who*
> > *could possibly descend into the underworld to*
> > *bring Christ up?," as if he had not been raised*
> > *from the dead!*
>
> But what does justification by faith declare to us? Again,
> in the words of the law:
>
> > *The message is near to you, well within your reach;*
> > *it is in your mouth to recite it and in your heart*
> > *to welcome it.*
>
> And this message is the gospel of justification by faith—
> proclaimed in the law but overlooked by Israel—which
> I too proclaim.—Romans 10:5-8

PRAYER    O God, you have not set me an impossible task. You
have not demanded that I demonstrate superhuman virtue or
power. You have done all that is necessary, for you have given me
Christ. For me to continue winning my own way into your good
graces, after you have set Christ so clearly before me, would be

worse than wrong-headed. It would be perversely rebellious. O Spirit, let me always follow your holy law with the strictest care. But never, never let me turn adherence to your law into a practical denial of the full sufficiency and ready accessibility of my Savior. O Christ, let my confidence in your infinite merit come to closure, to a decisive finality forever. Let me live from this moment on resting in the sufficiency of your merit alone. In your holy name. Amen.

> *Dwell much upon the necessity and excellency of that*
> *resting-place that God hath provided for you. Above*
> *all other resting-places, himself is your resting-place.*
> *His free mercy and love is your resting-place. The*
> *pure, glorious, matchless and spotless righteousness of*
> *Christ is your resting-place. Ah! It is sad to think that*
> *most men have forgotten their resting-place, as the*
> *Lord complains: "My people have been as lost sheep,*
> *their shepherds have caused them to go astray and*
> *have turned them away to the mountains. They are*
> *gone from mountain to hill and forgotten their resting-*
> *place" (Jeremiah 50:6). So poor souls that see not the*
> *excellency of that resting-place that God hath*
> *appointed for their souls to lie down in, they wander*
> *from mountain to hill, from one duty to another, and*
> *here they will rest and there they will rest. But souls*
> *that see the excellency of that resting-place that God*
> *hath provided for them, they will say, "Farewell*
> *prayer, farewell hearing, farewell fasting. I will rest no*
> *more in you, but now I will rest only in the bosom of*
> *Christ, the love of Christ, the righteousness of Christ."*
>
> *Thomas Brooks, 1608–1680*

❖   ❖   ❖

So what is justification telling us as it speaks through the law? It is explaining how saving faith manifests itself in someone's life. It is saying that you must declare plainly and publicly with your mouth your allegiance to Jesus as your only God and Master. And you must believe with a surrendering trust in your heart that God raised him from the dead, forever triumphant over evil, vindicated in all his claims and accepted by the Father in his atoning death. If you will respond to Christ, the true, full and glorious Christ, with this kind of faith, you will be saved.—Romans 10:9

**PRAYER**    O Lord God, your gospel is not as simple as some people would have me think, but neither is it as burdensome as others would have me undertake. I see that I cannot take Jesus as my Savior without also bowing before him as my Lord. And I also see that I cannot retain any lingering confidence in my own capacity for satisfying the demands of your law. Jesus is Lord. Let me never stop short of him. Jesus is Savior. Let me never go beyond him. Let me never trivialize the Son of God, one way or the other. Let me never send others down the wrong path as well. O God, let me be true to the gospel. Let me see your salvation. And let me bring many others along with me to a saving faith in Christ. In his holy name. Amen.

### A Confession of Personal Faith

*I confess that Jesus is Lord.*

*I confess that Jesus shares the name and the nature, the holiness, the authority, power, majesty and eternality of the one and only true God.*

*I confess that Jesus died and was raised, opening heaven up to unworthy sinners. I am such a sinner, and I gladly embrace his atonement for me.*

*I confess that Jesus rightfully owns me, every part of me,*
*every moment of my time, every dollar in my possession,*
*every opportunity granted me, every responsibility thrust*
*upon me, every hope I cherish, every person whom I love*
*and treasure. I am the personal property of the Lord*
*Jesus Christ. He deserves my allegiance, loyalty and trust*
*24 hours a day, in all places, in all aspects of my life, both*
*public and private. He is worthy of my obedience. He is*
*worthy of my utmost. He is worthy of my very blood.*

*I confess that Jesus is Lord.*

*Raymond C. Ortlund, Jr.*

❖   ❖   ❖

And why heart-belief and mouth-confession? Because
with the heart true faith is exercised, securing one's full
justification. And with the mouth open confession is
made, assuring one of eternal salvation. But even our
public confession of Christ arises from the impulse of
mere faith, for Scripture says, "No one who *trusts* in
Christ will regret it. Every believer's *faith* will be vindicated." And if faith is the stipulation, then justification
applies equally and universally to everyone alike without rank or distinction. The ethnic and cultural differences between a Jew and a Gentile do not limit the grace
of Christ, for one and the same Lord rules over us all,
showering the riches of his mercy upon all, with more
than enough to go around for all whose faith cries out
to him for salvation. As Scripture says, "Anyone at all
who calls on the name of the Lord Jesus will be
saved."—Romans 10:10-13

**PRAYER**     How small, O Lord, how petty, how self-serving, is
my natural concept of religion. It becomes just another way of
drawing the line between my own inner circle and everyone else.

It is no different from the mentality that makes the exclusive country club, the exclusive style, or the exclusive neighborhood the mark of social stature. And in the case of faith, I dare to put my own prejudice into your mouth as the authoritative Word of God, ranking one believer over another on a basis totally alien to the gospel itself. But underneath my self-promotion you see my insecurity, my restless unease with myself. Thank you, merciful Lord, for the wise gift of justification, for with one grace you banish two evils—the pride of exclusivism and the pain of self-contempt. Release me from my smallness, dear Lord, and use me to extend more widely the generous fellowship of the justified-by-faith-alone. In the holy name of Christ. Amen.

> *You yourself, once you are in the Inner Ring, want to make it hard for the next entrant, just as those who are already in made it hard for you. Naturally. In any wholesome group of people which holds together for a good purpose, the exclusions are in a sense accidental. But your genuine Inner Ring exists for exclusion. There'd be no fun if there were no outsiders. The invisible line would have no meaning unless most people were on the wrong side of it. Exclusion is no accident; it is the essence. The quest for the Inner Ring will break your heart, unless you break it.*
>
> C. S. Lewis, 1898–1963

❖   ❖   ❖

Moreover, God has provided for Israel not only a written witness to Christ in the law but a spoken witness as well, which they have also rejected—Romans 10:14-21

**All then that one must do to be saved is to call upon the Lord. But, of course, there are antecedent conditions nec-**

essary for this even to fall within the range of possibility. I mean, if people are to call on the Lord, they must have faith in him. And if they are to have faith in him, they must hear him. And if they are to hear him, there must be a messenger speaking for him. And if messengers are to speak for him, they must be sent by him. Now, has God failed to send Israel his duly authorized messengers of salvation? By no means. The Old Testament records their venturing forth: "How welcome a sound is the footfall of couriers bringing longed-for good news!" God *has* taken the initiative to convey the gospel to Israel, some of whom have welcomed it with joy—but, proportionately, only a few. Most have refused to submit to the gospel. This is why Isaiah agonizes in frustration: "O Lord, who has believed the message we have reported to them?" So then, a responsive faith is triggered by hearing the gospel, but hearing becomes effectual only when Christ himself is heard speaking through the gospel.—Romans 10:14-17

**PRAYER**     O Christ, how many sermons have I heard in my lifetime? How many times have I sat at your feet? And how many times have I slouched there bored, day-dreaming, distracted, sullen, surly and insolent? You have granted me thousands of opportunities to hear your voice, but how often have I really listened? O living Christ, let me see beyond the human messenger to discern your voice in the message. Let there be no famine of hearing the word of the Lord in me, in my church or in my generation. Shake us awake and speak to us again through your written Word. Let us hear your voice, living Lord. In your holy name. Amen.

*Question 160: What is required of those that hear the Word preached?*

*Answer: It is required of those that hear the Word preached that they attend upon it with diligence, preparation and prayer, examine what they hear by*

*the Scriptures, receive the truth with faith, love, meek-
ness and readiness of mind as the Word of God, meditate and confer of it, hide it in their hearts, and bring
forth the fruit of it in their lives.*

The Westminster Larger Catechism, *1648*

❖ ❖ ❖

But here is my point. Could it be alleged that Israel has
not called upon the Lord Jesus because they have not
heard the gospel? Is their failure of belief due to a lack of
exposure to the truth? Quite the contrary. The truth has
gone out far and wide:

> *The voice of God's messengers has gone forth
>     universally,
>     their words have penetrated to the remotest
>     corners of civilization.*

But let me press it further. Could it be argued that, even
if Israel has heard, they did not really understand the
message? No. Moses was only the first of many to deny
that excuse. God said through him:

> *I will make you green with envy by revealing
>     the Messiah to a nation that does not even
>     count in your estimation,
> I will spark your anger by speaking through
>     him to a nation you consider too backward
>     for spiritual insight.*

And neither can Israel plead that the Messiah could not
be found. Speaking for God, Isaiah has the nerve to say:

> *I was found by people who were not even
>     searching for me,
> I made myself obvious to those who were not
>     even looking for me.*

And then he tells Israel, "I have persistently, patiently, continually held out an invitation to my people, but they have refused me. They think they know better." Israel, therefore, is far from Christ not for lack of opportunity but for lack of responsiveness.—Romans 10:18-21

**PRAYER**    O Lord God, how comfortable we are. How exquisitely complacent. How deliciously at ease. We, your church, loll drowsily amid our privileges. We treat our spiritual treasures cheaply, as if possessing them in abundance were a natural state of affairs, always to be expected. We do not understand that they were developed for us out of the keen spiritual vitality and self-denial of past generations. We do not understand that we have no guarantee whatever that our privileges will always remain in our possession, for ourselves and our children after us. We do not understand that having the gospel preached in our churches, having Bibles in our hands, having worthy Christian literature, having faithful Christian schools and colleges and seminaries, having mission organizations and family counselors and all the many other avenues of grace that in fact we do possess—we do not understand that living amid abundant, God-given opportunity for richer spiritual life is not something to be taken for granted but something to be eagerly exploited. And if we do not exploit it, then why *shouldn't* you take it away and give it to others who will appreciate it? You watch us. You judge us. You evaluate our responsiveness to your gifts. You decide, accordingly, whether you will bestow more gifts upon us or remove what we have and turn it over to others—perhaps to others even less deserving, to shame us into repentance. O God, revive us again! Strip away our worldly distractions. Break the spell of our idolatrous affections. Infuse within our sinful hearts a vivid sense of the infinite worth and succulent pleasure of spiritual things. Let a new affection for you expel from within us our swinish preference for the earthly, the material, the sensate—as if you, *you*, were a colossal bore. *Whatever it takes*, make us a responsive people, before it is too late. In the holy name of Christ. Amen.

*Let me warn all careless members of churches to beware lest they trifle their souls into hell. You live on year after year as if there was no battle to be fought with sin, the world, and the devil. You pass through life a smiling, laughing, gentleman-like or lady-like person and behave as if there was no devil, no heaven and no hell. Oh, careless Churchman, or careless Dissenter, careless Episcopalian, careless Presbyterian, careless Independent, careless Baptist, awake to see eternal realities in their true light! Awake and put on the armor of God! Awake and fight hard for life! Tremble, tremble and repent.*

*J. C. Ryle, 1816–1900*

# ROMANS
## CHAPTER 11

ISRAEL'S UNBELIEF IS not without exception, however. God has preserved for himself a remnant of faithful Jews—Romans 11:1-10

So what should we conclude from Israel's condition?
That God has cancelled his relationship with them?
Unthinkable! Look at me. I am an Israelite, of the children of Abraham, of the tribe of Benjamin. *God has not
rejected his people,* whom he chose long ago. Or are you
unfamiliar with the story of Elijah? Scripture describes
how he pleads with God in accusation against Israel: "O
Lord, your people have murdered your prophets and
torn down your altars. I am the sole survivor of their
rampage, and they are coming after me as well." That is
how Elijah perceived the situation. But what was God's
answer to him? "I have preserved for myself seven thou-
sand men who have not submitted to disgusting Baal-
worship." This illustrates how, in our own day as well,
there is still a remnant of believing Jews, in keeping with
God's gracious choice. And since he chooses people by
the determining principle of grace, his selection of them

can no longer be considered a response to anything of
their own doing; otherwise, "grace" is twisted into something other than true grace. So the remnant exists not
because they are better than others but only because God
chose them—a symbol of hope for the nation's future.
—Romans 11:1-6

**PRAYER**    O Lord, how clever and persistent I am in my
attempts to intrude myself into the equation of grace. I would
even argue that it was something in me that you foresaw
which prompted you to choose me. I would argue my faith,
my repentance, my yearning for you, as possible grounds for
your choice of me. But I now repudiate it all. Why did I, a
hardened rebel, surrender my sword to you, my rightful King?
How did I, a lost wanderer, find my way to your doorstep?
Did I reason my way into your grace? Did I believe my way
there? Did I lift myself, fatally maimed, into your arms, my
Great Physician? No. It was your grace, and therefore your
choice. You alone framed the gracious plan according to
which I have come to be yours. You chose me for yourself,
and now you are preserving me for yourself. I yield fully to
you, omnipotent Savior. Only keep me faithful to yourself
amid the filthy idols of this present evil age. O God, preserve
me from sin. Lead me in the paths of righteousness, for your
name's sake, all the way home. In the holy name of Christ.
Amen.

> *I sought the Lord, and afterward I knew*
> *He moved my heart to seek him, seeking me.*
> *It was not I that found, O Savior true;*
> *No, I was found of thee.*

> *Thou didst reach forth thy hand and mine enfold.*
> *I walked and sank not on the storm-vexed sea.*

*'Twas not so much that I on thee took hold*
*As thou, dear Lord, on me.*

*I find, I walk, I love, but O the whole*
*Of love is but my answer, Lord, to thee,*
*For thou wert long beforehand with my soul;*
*Always thou lovedst me.*

*Anonymous, ca. 1878*

❖ ❖ ❖

So what is the outcome? The very favor Israel is so persistently seeking from God they have not obtained. But the chosen remnant has obtained it. As for the rest of the nation, they have been hardened in their unbelief. As it is written,

> *God has sent them into a spiritual coma,*
> *so that their eyes cannot see*
> *and their ears cannot hear,*
> *as it is to this day.*

And David says,

> *May the very blessings on which they feast*
> *become a snare and a trap,*
> *an obstacle and divine retribution for them.*
> *May their spiritual vision be darkened so that*
> *they cannot see,*
> *and may their back forever bend under the*
> *weight of their burden.*

—Romans 11:7-10

**PRAYER** O Living God, it is a fearful thing to fall into your hands. O Consuming Fire, let us worship you with all reverence and awe. We are sleepy and dull, bored and boring. O Source of all light and feeling and truth and joy, visit your church again with a spiritual awakening in our day. In a great act of sovereign grace, quicken our hearts to seek you without regard for the cost, and so to find you. Whatever else we must lose, let us recover you in all your glorious fullness, I pray, for there is nothing more wretched than our nominal religion, and there is nothing more fulfilling than your living presence among us. In the holy name of Christ. Amen.

*When is a revival necessary? . . . Wherever there are the proofs of spiritual death in or around the professing church, wherever there is an actual decay or dormancy in the energy or activity of its members, wherever there is the absence of a progression in those habits and feelings and principles that distinguish the divine life, there is a necessity for a revival. If, among those who profess a holy faith, we find a growing conformity to the world in its passions, its policy or its practices, a want of sensibility to the claims of God, to the glory of Jesus, or to the imperishable interests of immortal souls, a deadness in devotion, a lack of spirituality in sentiment and feeling, a willingness to parade a dwarfed and shrivelled Christianity before the world, as if it were the healthful and full-grown impersonation of a living and energetic faith, we say a revival is necessary. . . . When there are few conversions under the ministrations of the church, and souls are perishing around her, unpitied and unhelped, when there is an evident suspension or withdrawal of those spiritual influences that are alone efficient to convince or to comfort, when there is a visible defection from acknowledged principle or from attained piety, a cold, lukewarm formality usurping the place of a generous, devoted, living Christianity, we say that revival is required.*

*John MacNaughtan, 1807–1884*

❖  ❖  ❖

THE WAYS OF GOD with both Jews and Gentiles teach us humbly
to hope in his mercy and heedfully to fear his discipline
—Romans 11:11-24

So let me ask this: Unbelieving Israel has not stumbled
so as to fall and never rise again, have they? Unthinkable!
But their rejection of Christ *was* the occasion for salvation to come to the Gentiles. God has a purpose in this.
He aims to make Israel jealous, so that they might wake
up and claim Christ again for their own. But if Israel's
rejection of Christ thrusts his riches out into the rest of
the world, if their downfall means abundant blessing for
Gentiles, how much more will their full restoration
enrich the world! (Now what I am saying pertains
directly to you Gentile Christians. You may be surprised
to know that, as the apostle to the Gentiles, I esteem my
service as strategic also for the salvation of Jews. I pursue my ministry to you in the hope that I may kindle jeal-
ousy in the hearts of my people and so convert some of
them.) And if the Jews' fall from favor was instrumental
in sending the gospel of reconciliation to the whole
world, what will their readmittance to favor be but an
unprecedented quickening of spiritual life from the dead?
The believing remnant of Jews today is an elect token of
this glorious eventuality, for if the part of the dough
devoted to God as a firstfruits offering is holy, then the
whole batch must be holy as well. Israel's descent from
the patriarchs warrants the same expectation, for if the
root of the tree is holy, then the branches must be holy
as well.—Romans 11:11-16

PRAYER    O God of Abraham, Isaac and Jacob, how wicked,
prejudiced and blind your Christian church has sometimes been
toward the Jews. Some Christians, especially in previous ages,

have looked down on them with contempt and even hatred, as if they alone were responsible for the crucifixion of the Lord Jesus. No, Father, it was *our* sins, it was *my* sins, that nailed him there. Other Christians, especially in our present age, have failed the Jews by remaining silent about Christ, feeling overly cautious about sharing the gospel with them. We have not fulfilled your will that we make Israel jealous by our enjoyment of the promised Messiah. For these two sins, O Lord, forgive us. We long for the day when Christ will come again to heal all division. We long for the end of this present evil age and the final consummation of his kingdom. Until that moment of his awesome appearing, O Lord God, renew your church, that we may be a magnetic witness to all the nations. In the holy name of our Messiah. Amen.

> *Lo! He comes, with clouds descending,*
> *Once for favored sinners slain.*
> *Thousand, thousand saints attending*
> *Swell the triumph of his train.*
> *Alleluia! Alleluia! Alleluia!*
> *God appears on earth to reign.*
>
> *Every eye shall now behold him,*
> *Robed in dreadful majesty.*
> *Those who set at nought and sold him,*
> *Pierced and nailed him to the tree,*
> *Deeply wailing, deeply wailing, deeply wailing,*
> *Shall the true Messiah see.*
>
> *Now redemption, long expected,*
> *See in solemn pomp appear.*
> *All his saints, by man rejected,*
> *Now shall meet him in the air.*
> *Alleluia! Alleluia! Alleluia!*
> *See the day of God appear!*

*Yea, Amen! Let all adore thee,*
  *High on thine eternal throne.*
*Savior, take the power and glory.*
  *Claim the kingdom for thine own.*
*O come quickly! O come quickly!*
    *O come quickly!*
*Alleluia! Come, Lord, come!*

> John Cennick, 1718–1755;
> Charles Wesley, 1707–1788;
> Martin Madan, 1726–1790

✧ ✧ ✧

But let me develop that imagery. The covenant community can be thought of as a great olive tree, growing up through history from an Abrahamic root. Some of the branches, Jews unresponsive to Christ, have been broken off. But you, a Gentile Christian, a wild olive, have been grafted in among the remaining branches. Along with them, you have entered into the rich life of the root. So do not gloat over the Jewish branches! Remember that the life of the tree flows up to the branches from the root, not down from you to the root. The benefits you now enjoy stem from the covenants of the Old Testament. You may reply, "But Jewish branches were broken off to clear a place for me." Congratulations! And *why* were they broken off? Because of their unbelief. But you continue in your privileged position due only to your faith, not to any intrinsic superiority. So do not take an inflated view of yourself. Instead, tremble! If God did not exempt the natural branches from discipline, he will hardly exempt you, a grafted branch. Consider carefully God's kindness and severity—severity toward the Jews who have fallen away and his kindness toward you, *if* your faith continues steadfast in his kindness. Otherwise, you too will be cut off. And as for the Jewish branches, if they discontinue their unbelief, they will be grafted back in. God is quite capable of restoring them. After all, if you, a Gentile, have been cut out of your natural habitat as a wild olive branch and have been unnaturally grafted into a cultivated olive tree, how much more can God graft these natural, Jewish branches back into their own tree! You have no reason to feel superior, and they have no reason to despair.—Romans 11:17-24

**PRAYER**   O God, you have not given me my rich privileges in Christ to flatter my ego but to draw from me a deeper resolve humbly to obey you. Your kindness is meant to lead me to repentance. I do humble myself before you now. I am where I am only by your kindness, and I must continue steadfast there. In a way I do not fully understand, your sovereign choice of me does not make my faithfulness to you unnecessary. Somehow, your sovereign grace and my moral responsibility are both true, consistent and important. I therefore pray that you will sustain my dogged, painstaking, rugged pursuit of godliness every day, all my life long. But, Lord, the deceitfulness of my heart! I would rather pamper myself than discipline myself. I would rather look down on those who have fallen into sin than look to myself. Meet me in my darkness and never let me give up. Never let me fall away. Never let me discredit my faith. Let me begin well. Let me continue well. Let me die well. In your kindness, deliver me from resting on the pillow of a cost-free discipleship, for it would in fact cost me everything. In the holy name of Christ. Amen.

*"Simon, Simon, Satan hath desired to winnow thee as wheat"—here is our toil. "But I have prayed for thee, that thy faith may fail not"—this is our safety. ... His prayer must not exclude our labor.*

*Their thoughts are vain, who think that their watch-*
*ing can preserve the city which God himself is not*
*willing to keep. And are not theirs as vain, who think*
*that God will keep the city for which they themselves*
*are not careful to watch? . . . Surely, if we look to*
*stand in the faith of the sons of God, we must hourly,*
*continually, be providing and setting ourselves to*
*strive. It was not the meaning of our Lord and Savior*
*in saying, "Father, keep them in thy name," that we*
*should be careless to keep ourselves. To our own*
*safety, our own sedulity is required.*

*Richard Hooker, ca. 1554–1600*

✧  ✧  ✧

GOD'S PURPOSE IS, after a phase of disobedience for both Jews
and Gentiles alike, to show saving mercy to both Jews and
Gentiles alike—Romans 11:25-32

I am concerned, dear friends, that you Gentile believers
might give yourselves too much credit. I want you to see
the hidden divine purpose at work in the matters we
have been pondering. It is this: Israel has, in part, suffered spiritual paralysis, but only until such time as all
the Gentiles chosen for salvation have come to Christ. It
is in this way that all Israel will be saved. Just as it is
written,

*A Savior will come from Zion*
*who will remove all ungodliness from Jacob.*
*This is the covenant I will fulfill for them*
*at such time as I take away their sins.*

Because they have rejected the gospel, the Jews are
estranged from God, so that salvation has been dispersed
among you Gentiles. But because God chose them for his

own, they are still loved by him, since God will be true to his promises to the patriarchs. (This must be so, for God does not take back gifts given or cancel a call issued.) For just as you Gentiles were once disobedient to God but have now received mercy through the Jews' disobedience, so also it is now their turn to be disobedient so that they too may now receive the same mercy shown to you. What, then, have we learned of the ways of God? That God has so ordered history and our lives as to confine us all to a disobedience from which we could not escape, so that he could then bestow upon us all a mercy we could never deserve. His mercy triumphs over our disobedience.—Romans 11:25-32

**PRAYER**    You amaze me, Lord God. When your offer of salvation is spurned, you do not withdraw it. You extend it more widely. And then you come back to the first offer and ensure that it is eventually taken up. O God, when I see you most clearly, I see mercy. When I see your wrath, I see your mercy behind it. But when I see your mercy, I can discern nothing beyond, for mercy throbs at the very depths of your being. So this is where my faith comes finally to rest—in your mercy. I do not have all the answers to my questions about your sovereignty over me. But I do know that you will not betray my faith. You will not abandon me. You will not fail me. Truly, nothing will ever separate me from your love in Christ Jesus my Lord. You are a God whom I can trust with a full and final trust, because you are a God of sovereign mercy. I surrender myself to your mercy right now, confident that someday I will adore you with eternal seraphic fire blazing in my then sinless heart. In the holy name of Christ. Amen.

*When we fix ourselves upon the meditation and modulation of the mercy of God, even his judgments cannot put us out of tune, but we shall sing and be cheerful*

*even in them. . . . Let the devil make me so far desper-*
*ate as to conceive a time when there was no mercy, and*
*he hath made me so far an atheist. . . . If I despoil God*
*of his mercy any one minute and say, "Now God hath*
*no mercy," for that minute I discontinue his very*
*Godhead and his Being. . . . If some king of the earth*
*have so large an extent of dominion in north and south*
*that he hath winter and summer together in his domin-*
*ions, so large an extent east and west that he hath day*
*and night together in his dominions, much more hath*
*God mercy and judgment together. He brought light*
*out of darkness, not out of a lesser light. He can bring*
*thy summer out of winter, though thou have no spring,*
*though in the ways of fortune or understanding or con-*
*science thou have been benighted till now, wintered*
*and frozen, clouded and eclipsed, damped and*
*benumbed, smothered and stupefied till now. Now*
*God comes to thee. All occasions invite his mercies,*
*and all times are his seasons.*

*John Donne, 1573–1631*

❖   ❖   ❖

THE ONLY FITTING RESPONSE to this display of God's sovereignty in
mercy and judgment is to bow in adoration—Romans 11:33-36

O the immensity of the wealth of God's mercy! O the
profundity of the wisdom of his purpose! O the infalli-
bility of his knowledge of all things! How his decrees
transcend our understanding and his ways defeat our
attempts to comprehend!

*For who sees reality from the Lord's perspective?*
*Or to whom has he ever turned for advice?*
*Or who has ever provided God with anything*
*so that God must respond as man's equal?*

For from him as sovereign Initiator and through him as faithful Sustainer and for him as worthy Goal is the totality of history! To him be the glory forever! Amen.
—Romans 11:33-36

**PRAYER**    O infinite God, you conceal within yourself the final explanation of life's mysteries. For this I trust you. You execute your will in my life without my help. For this I rest in you. You sanctify all events with divine meaning and purpose, so that I am always safe, no matter what evil befalls me. For this I rejoice in you. With you there, O God, being who you are, everything ultimately will be all right, because all things are moving toward your glory. O God and Father, be glorified here on the platform of my little life, for your glory is my eternal security and everlasting joy. In the holy name of Christ. Amen.

> *My God, how wonderful thou art,*
> *Thy majesty how bright!*
> *How beautiful thy mercy-seat*
> *In depths of burning light!*
>
> *How dread are thine eternal years,*
> *O everlasting Lord,*
> *By prostrate spirits day and night*
> *Incessantly adored!*
>
> *O how I fear thee, living God,*
> *With deepest, tenderest fears,*
> *And worship thee with trembling hope*
> *And penitential tears!*
>
> *Yet I may love thee too, O Lord,*
> *Almighty as thou art,*
> *For thou hast stooped to ask of me*
> *The love of my poor heart.*

*How beautiful, how beautiful,*
  *The sight of thee must be,*
*Thine endless wisdom, boundless power*
  *And awesome purity!*

      *Frederick William Faber, 1814–1863*

# ROMANS

## CHAPTER 12

THE APPLICATION OF THE GOSPEL—ROMANS 12:1-15:13

THE ONLY RESPONSE to the gospel consistent with the gospel itself
is to yield oneself fully to God and grow into a new life of holiness
—Romans 12:1-2

> Having spread before you, dear friends, the mercies of
> God, I now call you to offer your whole selves to him as
> a sacrifice alive with new life, set apart by holiness,
> pleasing to God. Such an act of worship is the only mean-
> ingful response to the gospel. Resist being stamped by the
> views and values of this passing age. Break with the
> world. Open your hearts to a radically new outlook on
> life through a reorientation of your thinking and affec-
> tions. If you will, God will equip you with discernment
> and quicken you with desire for living out his will—that
> which is morally good, pleasing to him and completely
> devoted.—Romans 12:1-2

**PRAYER**     O Lord, you have shown me your glory, bright with your sovereignty, your mercy, your justice, with your overruling of my sin by an invincible salvation, with your assurances of a love that will never cast me off, with your promises of eternal joys yet to come. And now you confront me. I have no right to be indifferent to your mercies. The only way forward into a new life with you is through the complete surrender that true faith always entails. This is right. A nominal faith is unworthy of you. It insults you. Love so amazing, so divine, demands my soul, my life, my all. And so I am telling you right now, dear Lord, that you have me. All of me. I hereby consecrate myself to a life of unworldly love, with you at the center. Remake me, according to your will. In the holy name of Christ. Amen.

> *I have been before God, and have given myself, all that I am and have, to God, so that I am not in any respect my own. I can challenge no right in this understanding, this will, these affections, which are in me. Neither have I any right to this body or any of its members—no right to this tongue, these hands, these feet, no right to these senses, these eyes, these ears, this smell or this taste. I have given myself clear away, and have not retained anything as my own. I have this morning told him that I did take him for my whole portion and felicity, looking on nothing else as any part of my happiness, nor acting as if it were, and his law for the constant rule of my obedience, and would fight with all my might against the world, the flesh and the devil to the end of my life, and that I did believe in Jesus Christ and did receive him as a Prince and Savior, and that I would adhere to the faith and obedience of the gospel, however hazardous and difficult the confession and practice of it may be, and that I did receive the blessed Spirit as my Teacher, Sanctifier and only Comforter, and cherish all his motions to enlighten, purify, confirm, comfort and assist me. This I have done. And I pray God, for the sake*

*of Christ, to look upon it as a self-dedication and to*
*receive me now as entirely his own and to deal with me in*
*all respects as such, whether he afflicts me or prospers me*
*or whatever he pleases to do with me.*

*Jonathan Edwards, January 12, 1723*

❖   ❖   ❖

THE GOSPEL CALLS US to fit humbly and actively into the church,
wherever each of us belongs—Romans 12:3-8

As one privileged with apostolic office, I tell each of you
this: Do not cherish an exaggerated view of your own
importance, your own gifts and your own entitlements.
That would be contrary to the realism required by the
gospel. Instead, think your way to a levelheaded view of
yourself, in keeping with the standard of self-assessment
God has given you in your faith. This down-to-earth esti-
mate of ourselves will bring us together as the church, for
we are like a body. And even as the human body has many
parts, each with its own special function, so all of us are
one body together in Christ, each of us vitally connected
with the others. We should make good use of the various
gifts God has graciously given us. If your gift is prophecy,
then exercise it within the parameters of your faith. If
your gift is serving, then serve. If you are a teacher, then
teach. Encouragers should encourage, givers should be
selfless, leaders should be energetic, and those who show
mercy should work gladly.—Romans 12:3-8

PRAYER    Lord Jesus Christ, if you are willing to own the
church as yours, how can I stand aloof? If you are active within
it, how can I withhold involvement? I thrill to the vision of your
church as that holy catholic army marching through history, triumphant over her foes. But the particular churches I see around

me hardly match that glorious vision. And a streak of pride runs deep within me, choking fellowship at its root. Forgive me, Lord. Along with the spiritual gift you have graciously given me, impart to me as well the humility to put that gift to work in fruitful partnership with the ministry of my church. In your holy name. Amen.

> *A proud man is unsatisfied with his standing in communion with the church of Christ and is either ambitiously aspiring to a dominion over it or is inclined to a separation from it. They are too good to stand on even ground with their brethren. They must be of some more refined or elevated society.*
>
> *Richard Baxter, 1615–1691*

❖ ❖ ❖

THE GOSPEL CALLS US to pursue the virtues of love, both for our fellow Christians and for those who oppose the gospel's claim upon our lives—Romans 12:9-21

> When their lives demonstrate real love, this is what Christians look like: They utterly reject evil. They cling devotedly to good. They cherish one another in brotherly love. Rather than compete for first place, they promote one another. When earnest effort is called for, they do not hold back. They radiate the presence of the Holy Spirit. They actively serve the Lord. They are lifted by hope above circumstances into joy. They remain steadfast under stress. They are persistently devoted to prayer. They are generously responsive to the needs of God's people. They seek out opportunities to show hospitality in their homes.—Romans 12:9-13

PRAYER    O God of love, your mercies have claimed me, and I have surrendered. You now call me to follow you in pouring myself out for others in a lifelong series of thousands of small gestures of love, various in form and wide in distribution. Yes, Lord, I affirm your command. Give me now the privilege of obedience. Deliver me from big-talking, self-congratulatory good intentions which feel so good but bear no fruit, and impart to me the qualities of a real, working love. Enable what you command, O Lord, and command whatever you wish. In the holy name of Christ. Amen.

> But that which was most sad and lamentable was that in two or three months' time half of their company died, especially in January and February, being the depth of winter, and wanting houses and other comforts, being infected with the scurvy and other diseases which this long voyage and their inaccommodate condition had brought on them. So as there died sometimes two or three of a day in the foresaid time, that of one hundred and odd persons, scarce fifty remained. And of these, in the time of most distress, there were but six or seven sound persons who to their great commendations, be it spoken, spared no pains night nor day, but with abundance of toil and hazard of their own health, fetched them wood, made them fires, dressed them meat, made their beds, washed their loathsome clothes, clothed and unclothed them. In a word, did all the homely and necessary offices for them which dainty and queasy stomachs cannot endure to hear named; and all this willingly and cheerfully, without any grudging in the least, showing herein their true love unto their friends and brethren, a rare example and worthy to be remembered. . . . And I doubt not but their recompense is with the Lord.
>
> William Bradford,
> recalling the first winter
> for the Pilgrims in New England,
> 1620-1621

✧  ✧  ✧

Pray God's blessing upon those who persecute you. Do not curse them, bless them. Show sympathy of feeling with others, weeping with those who are sad and being happy for those who are glad. Let a spirit of oneness bind you together with all believers. Do not be snobbish, but enjoy the company of ordinary people. Do not overrate yourselves. Do not insist on settling scores, evil for evil. Rather than retaliate, consider carefully how to display the highest ideals before others. If possible, as far as it depends on you, live peacefully with everyone. But when your efforts fail, do not seek revenge for yourselves, dear friends. Instead, allow for God's wrath to take its own course. It is written, "The righting of wrongs is my prerogative. I will settle all scores," says the Lord. By contrast, our part is to love our enemy. "If he is hungry, feed him. If he is thirsty, give him a drink. When you respond to his hostility in this way, you will make his conscience burn with shame." Refuse to be drawn into the vicious cycle of evil-for-evil. Even if you are in the right, you will soon be ensnared in the wrong and thus defeated. Instead, you go on the offensive and defeat evil by responding to it with good.—Romans 12:14-21

**PRAYER**    O my Lord, life in the gospel follows the way of the cross. It entails conflict. Inevitably it must, not because I want it so but because the world I live in has surrendered to your enemy and embraced his demonic values. I am often opposed, Lord, not in the fire or on the rack but in assaults and tortures almost invisible to everyone but the one targeted. But you understand my anguish, for you yourself endured suffering at the hands of evil men. And you did not retaliate. Their shrieking hatred was met by your gracious dignity. You did not even open your mouth. Lord, you lost.

And yet you won, for you stuck to what was right and kept entrusting your case to God. And will not the Judge of all the earth do right? I would rather lose with you, dear Lord, than win with the world. Let them have their nasty little victories. But, my Lord, in your mercy enable me to keep trusting you enough to walk strictly in your ways, even when it costs my earthly possessions, privileges and comforts. I want a conquest this world can neither give to me nor steal from me. Let me overcome evil with good. Let me never lash out, as if I had no heavenly Defender standing up for me. Let me lose now, if I have to, so that I may hear your "Well done" then. In your holy name. Amen.

*Workman of God, O lose not heart,*
*But learn what God is like,*
*And in the darkest battlefield*
*Thou shalt know where to strike.*

*Thrice blest is he to whom is given*
*The instinct that can tell*
*That God is on the field when he*
*Is most invisible.*

*He hides himself so wondrously,*
*As though there were no God.*
*He is least seen when all the powers*
*Of ill are most abroad.*

*Ah! God is other than we think;*
*His ways are far above,*
*Far beyond reason's height, and reached*
*Only by childlike love.*

*Then learn to scorn the praise of men,*
  *And learn to lose with God.*
*For Jesus won the world through shame,*
  *And beckons thee his road.*

*For right is right, since God is God,*
  *And right the day must win.*
*To doubt would be disloyalty,*
  *To falter would be sin.*

*Frederick William Faber, 1814–1863*

# ROMANS

## CHAPTER 13

OUR LIFE OF GOSPEL SURRENDER also entails a cooperative
spirit toward civil government—Romans 13:1-7

Every one of us is obliged to be properly dutiful to the
civil authorities over us, because no authority exists
except by the will of God, and the government currently
in power has been ordained by God. So anyone unwill-
ing to submit to authority has taken a stand against a
divine institution. Such rebels will pull down judgment
upon themselves. Moreover, governmental rulers do not
frighten honest citizens but only lawbreakers. Would you
like not to live in fear of the government? Do what is
right, and you will be commended. For government is a
servant of God, intended for your benefit, enforcing
order so that you can do good with your life. But if you
do evil, you have ample reason to fear. The government
does not bear the sword for nothing! It serves God's
wrath by punishing evildoers. Therefore, a proper submission is required of us not only because we fear trouble but also, a higher reason, because we want to keep a

clear conscience. This is why we pay taxes. Public offi-
cials are serving a God-ordained function by running the
government. So fulfill your obligations to all by paying
taxes, revenues, respect or honor, each as it is properly
due.—Romans 13:1-7

**PRAYER**    O my God and King, you love order. You have
undertaken to establish order, both in the universe and here on
earth in human society. But I find in my heart an anarchic
impulse, an autonomous conceit, defiant even of legitimate
authority. I resent all limitation imposed upon me. My ego cannot endure that there is something superior in this universe to
Self. I see this most vividly in relation to you, but also in relation
to those lower authorities you have established over me, including human government. Your orderly ranking of powers over me
can feel more like a crushing burden than a benevolent position-
ing of me where I can flourish without destroying others or
myself. I confess my seditious spirit. I confess that you are
supreme and I am not. I surrender to the order you have struc-
tured for me. Teach me what it means to be a Christian here
within this network of earthly obligations. Let me keep my conscience clear before you, both by obeying the state with an
ungrudging deference when its demands are lawful and by defying the state with a holy detachment when its demands are idolatrous. O God, let your church in this generation be so fully
surrendered to you that we rise above both compromise and
fanaticism. Keep vividly before us your promise of the new
earth, where alone righteousness dwells. In the holy name of
Christ. Amen.

> You ask me what I shall do if I am called by the
> emperor. I will go even if I am too sick to stand on my
> feet. If Caesar calls me, God calls me. If violence is
> used, as well it may be, I commend my cause to God.

*He lives and reigns who saved the three youths from the fiery furnace of the king of Babylon. And if he will not save me, my head is worth nothing compared with Christ. This is no time to think of safety. I must take care that the gospel is not brought into contempt by our fear to confess and seal our teaching with our blood.*

*Martin Luther, 1520*

✧ ✧ ✧

LOVE IS TO BE the pervasive flavor of gospel living
—Romans 13:8-10

Leave no human obligation unmet. Love, however, is by its nature a responsibility incapable of being exhausted. Love is the message of God's law, for the one who loves his neighbor has fulfilled what the law demands. Think of the commandments: "You must not commit adultery. You must not kill. You must not steal. You must not envy," and the others. The essence of them all is expressed in this one rule: "Your love must care no less about the next person than you care about yourself." Such love will never violate another person. And that is why love is the true meaning and practical fulfillment of the law.—Romans 13:8-10

PRAYER   O Lord, your gospel calls me to brokenness, to yieldedness, to surrender. As I stand here before you, indebted to mercy, loved into submission, you now call me to live a higher life by the power of your Holy Spirit. You call me away from my natural opportunism and cynicism, away from unprincipled self-promotion and self-display, to conscience, to consideration, to the love commanded by your holy law. You call me to sincerity and kindness and patience and courtesy and all the simple virtues that arrogant social engineers have no time for but which truly change the world. O Lord, let my life rise above the race to be the first to the trough and instead be flavored throughout by a visible and winsome regard for others. This is my debt to your own infinite love for me, a debt I can never repay in full. Do not let my selfish heart fail to give you at least something in return for the riches you have poured out on me, dear Lord. In the holy name of Christ. Amen.

*O God our Father, throned on high,*
*Enrobed in ageless splendor,*
*To thee, in awe and love and joy,*
*Ourselves we would surrender—*
*To live obedient to thy will*
*As servants to each other,*
*And show our faithfulness to thee*
*By love to one another.*

*To serve by love! O teach us how.*
*Be this our great vocation—*
*To comfort grief, to seek the lost*
*With message of salvation.*
*In loving may our full hearts beat,*
*Our words be wise and winning.*
*In helping others may our joy*
*Have ever new beginning.*

*Thee, Lord, for thy dear Son we bless;*
*His heart for us was broken.*
*O Love, upon the bitter cross*
*Thy deepest word was spoken!*
*The echo of that word is heard*
*In love for every brother.*
*So test we, Lord, our love for thee*
*By loving one another.*

*George Thomas Coster, 1835–1912*

❖ ❖ ❖

THE GOSPEL WARNS US that we have little time left to clean up our lives and become fit for Christ's return—Romans 13:11-14

> Realize the significance of the moment. It is high time for you to wake up from your lethargic, leisurely living! As time runs out, our coming salvation is ever nearer to us than it was when we became Christians. The night of sin still hangs over this world, but it is almost over. The day we long for has drawn near. Therefore, change is in order! Let us throw off as old rags those things we do that belong to the darkness. And let us outfit ourselves with armor from God's arsenal of light and holiness. Let us live now, even in the lingering darkness, as in broad daylight, honorably, with nothing to hide. Let us leave behind in the darkness, where they belong, wild parties and drunken binges, sexual affairs and fast living, quarreling and jealousy. Instead, adorn your lives with all the virtues and graces of the Lord Jesus Christ, and offer your old nature no opportunity to gratify its desires.
> —Romans 13:11-14

PRAYER    Almighty King, come and dispel the crushing darkness of this present evil age. Violence, sensuality, gaudiness, noise, stupidity, arrogance, cruelty, weirdness, misery, loneliness, vulgarity, shallowness, hypocrisy, irreverence, blasphemy, lies, heresy—darkness, darkness, darkness! I am often sick at heart with it. O Lord, how long? Come and build the perfect world we have always attempted and have always perverted. Build your own kingdom, bursting with life and holiness and truth and joy and wholesomeness and simplicity and wisdom and humility and laughter and worship and peace and knowledge and depth and meaning and harmony, to your universal honor and glory. You have promised that you will. Nothing stands in your way. It is only the Father's timing, not any human power, that restrains you from coming this very moment. O Lord, teach me to live on the edge of eternity. Never let me lie at ease in peace when there is no peace. Shake me awake. Stand me on my feet. Put a sword in my hand. And let me fight nobly until the day of your appearing, sealing my testimony to you with the wounds of my warfare. In your holy name. Amen.

*It may be you are struggling hard for the rewards of this world. Perhaps you are straining every nerve to obtain money or place or power or pleasure. If that be your case, take care. Your sowing will lead to a crop of bitter disappointment. Unless you mind what you are about, your latter end will be to lie down in sorrow. Thousands have trodden the path you are pursuing, and have awoke too late to find it end in misery and eternal ruin. They have fought hard for wealth and honor and office and promotion and turned their backs on God and Christ and heaven and the world to come. And what has their end been? Often, far too often, they have found out that their whole life has been a grand mistake. . . . For your own happiness' sake, resolve this day to join the Lord's side. Shake off your past carelessness and unbelief. Come out from the ways of a thoughtless, unreasoning world. Take up the cross and become a good soldier of Christ. . . . Awake to a sense of the misery of being a slave. For life and happiness and liberty, arise and fight.*

*J. C. Ryle, 1816–1900*

# ROMANS

## CHAPTER 14

THE LIFE OF GOSPEL SURRENDER calls us to accept other believers
when they differ from us in matters of personal opinion—
Romans 14:1-12

Welcome into your fellowship the believer whose faith
has not yet grown strong enough to enjoy the liberty
opened up by free justification. And in receiving such
a one, do not require that your disagreements be settled. For example, one Christian's faith allows him to
eat all kinds of foods, while another Christian is a veg-
etarian. But your respect for one another is more
important than your differences. So the one who eats
whatever he likes must not despise the other, and the
one who restricts his diet must not condemn the other,
because *God* has welcomed each one into the fellowship. Who are *you* to set the standard of acceptability
for Someone Else's servant? It is up to his Master, not
you, to determine the acceptability or unacceptability
of his service. And each servant will be acceptable,
because the Master is able to make him acceptable in

the things that matter. Or there is also the question of days. One Christian esteems one day more than another, while the next Christian considers every day the same. But more important than the disagreement itself is the necessity that each of us form a settled personal conviction. That way, even if we are mistaken, the governing principle of our lives will still fit the ultimate Christian criterion—living for the Lord. So the one who observes a certain day as holy does so for the Lord. The one who eats whatever he likes does so for the Lord, giving God thanks. And the one who restricts his diet does so for the Lord, giving God thanks no less. Look at it from the larger perspective. None of us lives for self. None of us dies for self. As long as we live, our living serves the Lord. And when we come to die, our dying serves the Lord. In both living and dying we are in the service of the Lord. It was for this very purpose that Christ died and sprang again to life—that *he* would reign as Lord over both the dead and the living. What warrant then do *you* have for condemning your brother? Or you there, what warrant do *you* have for despising your brother? Judgment is indeed in order— when we *all* stand before the judgment seat of God! For it is written,

> *As certain it is as my very existence, says the Lord—*
> *every knee will bend to me in submission,*
> *and every tongue will make to God its confession.*

Yes, each of us will give an account of himself to God.
—Romans 14:1-12

**PRAYER**  O Lord, even while we believers stand together as your church, in a deeper sense each of us stands alone before you. Each of us bows personally to your Lordship over the whole of life. We live before you. We die before you. I stand before you at this moment. I am no longer my own, to shape my life as I please. I have been bought with a price. You own me, every bit of me. Whatever happens to me, it serves your purpose for my existence. And my subordination to your rule is not something I have generously awarded you. You won it for yourself at the cross and the empty tomb. Be well served by my life. Be well served by my death. And, O Lord, keep vividly before me that solemn moment when I will leave this world and answer to you at your judgment seat for the way I have lived and died. Let me live now, let me die now, for you and you alone, so that I may meet you there with unmixed joy. In your holy name. Amen.

*But we will never give ourselves to the Lord, till we consider what he hath done for us. He hath given himself wholly for us, left heaven for us, denied himself for us, made himself of no reputation for us, became a worm and no man, a curse for us. And in way of requital, we should answer him with giving ourselves and all we have to him. This is to be a Christian to purpose. Christ hath given himself to me, and therefore I will give my goods, myself, my life to Christ. . . . I am not mine own; he hath myself. . . . He shall have whatsoever is mine. If he call me to suffer losses, crosses, disgrace or death itself, welcome all. I am his, and therefore whatsoever is mine is his. And it is no more than he hath done for me. . . . And therefore the martyrs were willing to part with their lives. . . . The reason is, which I desire not to be forgotten, we have a better being in God than in ourselves. If we lose our natural life, we have in him a better life. If we lose our riches, we have them in heavenly treasures. The water is not lost that runneth into the sea. It is in the ocean still, its better receptacle.*

*Richard Sibbes, 1577–1635*

✧ ✧ ✧

THE LIFE OF GOSPEL SURRENDER forbids us to enjoy our freedom
heedless of its effect upon other believers—Romans 14:13-23

> Our accountability to God means, then, that we must
> stop condemning one another in these merely personal
> matters. Instead, let this principle be your policy—never
> to impede or hinder a fellow Christian in his walk of
> faith. (Personally, I am totally convinced, on the author-
> ity of the Lord Jesus, that none of these disputed things
> is intrinsically unclean. But any one of them becomes
> virtually unclean for the Christian whose conscience
> considers it so.) If your brother suffers anguish because
> of what you eat, your exercise of a legitimate freedom
> has failed to meet the higher test of love. Do not ruin one
> for whom Christ died for the sake of your mouthful of
> food. Do not let the freedom of the gospel, a good thing
> in itself and a benefit to you, be slandered due to your
> abuse of it. For the kingdom of God becomes clearly
> manifest not when Christians insist on pleasing them-
> selves with their food and drink but when their lives
> demonstrate righteousness and peace and joy in the
> Holy Spirit. That is why the believer who serves Christ
> with such graciousness of life is a delight to God and
> convincing to man. So then, let us work hard at devel-
> oping a relational atmosphere conducive to harmony
> and growth together. Do not undo what God is doing in
> other believers' lives for the sake of mere food. Yes, all
> foods are clean. But it is wrong to exercise this freedom
> indifferent to the problems it creates for others. The
> right thing to do is not to eat foods or drink wine or do
> other things which could work mischief in the life of a
> fellow believer. If *you* have a strong faith, enjoy it in per-
> sonal communion with God, not in causing trouble for
> other Christians. Blessed is the one whose conscience

does not cast doubt on the choices he makes. But the one who is unsure when he eats something stands condemned in the very act, because his eating has taken his conscience out further than his faith can support him. Every use of freedom which is not rooted in one's real faith is a sin.—Romans 14:13-23

**PRAYER**    O my Lord, let me never be morally reckless. Let me never force my conscience, for this is surely the first step in the direction of total ruin. If I am willing to take that one step, then I have forfeited any reason not to take the next one, and then the next one. O Lord, let me reverence conscience, in myself and in others. Let me reverence duty and right, especially in this wildly careless age in which I live. Create in me and in your church a sense of profound respect for questions of conscience. We are so lax. We have nothing of a watchman mentality. We trumpet our freedom in the gospel, but our living looks more like an easygoing indifference to matters of right and wrong. Lord, we even feel *superior* to previous generations of believers, who at least took moral questions seriously. We view their faith as strict and narrow. But we ourselves are so soft, so casually compliant, so unthinking and undiscerning and uncaring, we are no different from the world around us. We are the influenced, not the influential, because our faith has no moral power, no unbending resolve, no heroic defiance grounded in profoundly held personal conviction. O Lord, awaken us! Enlighten our darkness. Sensitize our dullness. Give us backbone. The world will never be won by Christians like us. We need hearts alert to the right, jealously guarding peace of conscience, whatever the personal cost. We need consciences that would rather *die* than compromise with evil. O Jesus our Righteousness, forgive us for trivializing our moral decisions. Quicken our yearnings for unstained integrity in every detail of life. In your holy name. Amen.

*Your Imperial Majesty and Your Lordships demand a simple answer. Here it is, plain and unvarnished. Unless I am convinced of error by Scripture and plain reason, my conscience is captive to the Word of God. I cannot and will not recant anything. For to go against conscience is neither right nor safe. Here I stand. I can do no other. God help me. Amen.*

Martin Luther, 1521

# ROMANS

## CHAPTER 15

THE LIFE OF GOSPEL SURRENDER moderates the demands of self, so that the church can, with united voice, glorify God —Romans 15:1-6

Now we who are able to exercise the freedom of faith must bear the burdens and inconveniences caused by the weaknesses of other believers who are still unable to venture forth in their freedom. We must not live to please ourselves only, selfishly ignoring others. Each of us should try to please the next person, aiming at the other's true benefit, and the church will grow strong. For not even Christ lived to please himself but was so consumed with a purpose higher than self that he willingly suffered for it. As it is written, "The insults they aimed at you, O God, hit me." This verse speaks to us as well. Indeed, everything written in the Old Testament was meant to teach us. And the lesson we are to learn is that, drawing steadfastness and encouragement from the Scriptures, we should hold fast to the glorious hope out ahead of us and not give up. Now may the God who gives this steadfastness and

encouragement grant that you all, both strong and weak, be bound together with unity of spirit, in obedience to Christ Jesus, so that you lift a unanimous voice of praise to the God and Father of our Lord Jesus Christ.
—Romans 15:1-6

**PRAYER**    O Father in heaven, I pray for the unity of your church. I do not ask for a thin, cheap unity made easy by a lack of strong convictions among believers, a unity of the sort we see at times among people in our relativistic society. That would be unworthy of your name. But I do ask for a unity which esteems the call of the gospel so highly that self is demoted for the common good. I ask for a unity which honors doctrine, a unity which follows the example of Christ, a unity agreeable with high Christian principle. We are not capable of this, dear God. We are too weak. We gravitate either toward a firm stand for doctrine alone or toward a soft relationalism without strong content. But to be like Jesus, who never compromised truth and who never violated the meaning of love—this takes us far beyond our capacities. O blessed Spirit, fill us moment by moment, lifting us up out of our natural littleness to a love worthy of the name. O Lord, translate the communion of saints from our creed into our hearts, that your church may with one voice lift great volumes of praise to our God and Father. In your holy name. Amen.

*Now, if we are called upon to love our neighbor as ourselves when he is not a Christian, how much more . . . should there be beauty in the relationships between true Bible-believing Christians, something so beautiful that the world would be brought up short! We must hold our distinctives. Some of us are Baptists; some of us hold to infant baptism; some of us are Lutheran, and so on. But to true Bible-believing Christians across*

*all the lines, in all the camps, I emphasize: if we do not
show beauty in the way we treat each other, then in the
eyes of the world and in the eyes of our own children,
we are destroying the truth we proclaim. . . . My
favorite church in Acts and, I guess, in all of history is
the church at Antioch. . . . It was a place where something new happened: the great, proud Jews who
despised the Gentiles . . . came to a break-through.
They could not be silent. They told their Gentile neigh-
bors about the gospel, and suddenly, on the basis of the
blood of Christ and the truth of the Word of God, the
racial thing was solved. There were Jewish Christians
and there were Gentile Christians, and they were one!
. . . The church at Antioch on the basis of the blood of
Christ encompassed the whole. There was a beauty
that the Greek and the Roman world did not know—
and the world looked.*

*Francis Schaeffer, 1912–1984*

✧   ✧   ✧

UNITY OF HEART with all true Christians is mandatory as a necessary implication of the gospel itself—Romans 15:7-13

Since you have this exalted purpose of glorifying God
together, welcome one another with open hearts, just as
Christ welcomed you, for the glory of God. For I assert
that Christ has become Servant to Jews out of God's
faithfulness, to fulfill the covenant promises God made
to the patriarchs. And, no less, Christ has become
Servant to Gentiles out of God's mercy, so that they glorify God. As it is written,

*For this I will confess you among the Gentiles,
and I will sing praises to your name.*

Furthermore, the Scripture also says,

> *Make merry, O Gentiles, along with God's people!*

Moreover, it says,

> *Praise the Lord, all you Gentiles,*
> *and may all the nations praise him!*

Additionally, Isaiah says,

> *A Davidic shoot will grow out of Jesse;*
> *he will rise up to rule the Gentiles,*
> *and they will put their hope in him.*

—Romans 15:7-12

**PRAYER**    O Christ, your gospel defines your church. We do not. You determine whom you will receive into your fellowship. We do not. You have welcomed all believers to yourself (some of whom *I* would *never* have invited in) on the same terms. You have granted all believers the same privileges of salvation. None of us has the right to impose conditions for fellowship which you do not require. Your gospel, therefore, is the great unifying force in the church. To the degree that we understand and believe the gospel, we will be one. To the degree that we honor you, we will be one. But to the degree that we exclude your true people from our hearts, we exclude you and deny your gospel. O living Christ, let the unifying power of the gospel sweep away our many divisions and bring your people together as one, to your greater glory in the world. In your holy name. Amen.

> *When is it Christians all agree*
> *And let distinctions fall?*
> *When, nothing in themselves, they see*
> *That Christ is all in all.*

*But strife and difference will subsist*
*While men will something seem.*
*Let them but singly look to Christ,*
*And all are one in him.*

*The infant and the aged saint,*
*The worker and the weak,*
*They who are strong and seldom faint,*
*And they who scarce can speak.*

*Eternal life's the gift of God.*
*It comes through Christ alone.*
*'Tis his, he bought it with his blood,*
*And therefore gives his own.*

*We have no life, no power, no faith,*
*But what by Christ is given.*
*We all deserve eternal death,*
*And thus we all are even.*

*Joseph Hart, 1712–1768*

❖   ❖   ❖

Now may the God who imparts this hope to your hearts
fill you all with an abundance of joy and peace as you live
out your faith together, so that you grow vigorous with
this irrepressible hope, by the power of the Holy Spirit.
—Romans 15:13

PRAYER    What wisdom and tenderness you show, dear Lord,
in the way you draw us out of self and into the communion of
saints. You do not coerce us, although you could. You do not
organize an ecclesiastical bureaucracy to enforce our compliance,
although you could. Instead, you win us and melt us. You lead
us out of the prison of self with hope. O dear Lord, fill your

church with all joy and peace and an abundance of hope today, amid the surrounding fear and despair. Let us not run from life but live well in it. Lift our eyes to higher things, heavenly things, far above the crime in our neighborhoods and the filth on our televisions and the cynicism of our politics. Lift our eyes above this blood-soaked earth to your kingdom above. Lift our eyes to the hills from whence comes our help. O dear Lord, fill your church in these hard times with the sweet, bright affections of your glorious gospel, that others might be drawn in by the magnetism of our hope. In your holy name. Amen.

> *In Kiev, where I found myself on a Sunday morning, on an impulse I turned into a church where a service was in progress. It was packed tight, but I managed to squeeze myself against a pillar whence I could survey the congregation and look up at the altar. Young and old, peasants and townsmen, parents and children, even a few in uniform—it was a variegated assembly. The bearded priests, swinging their incense, intoning their prayers, seemed very remote and far away. Never before or since have I participated in such worship; the sense conveyed of turning to God in great affliction was overpowering. Though I could not, of course, follow the service, I knew from Klavdia Lvovna little bits of it; for instance, where the congregation say there is no help for them save from God. What intense feeling they put into these words! In their minds, I knew, as in mine, was a picture of those desolate abandoned villages, of the hunger and the hopelessness, of the cattle trucks being loaded with humans in the dawn light. Where were they to turn for help? Not to the Kremlin, and the Dictatorship of the Proletariat, certainly; nor to the forces of progress and democracy and enlightenment in the West. . . . Every possible human agency found wanting. So, only God remained, and to God*

*they turned with a passion, a dedication, a humility,*
*impossible to convey. They took me with them. I felt*
*closer to God then than I ever had before, or am likely*
*to again.*

> Malcolm Muggeridge, 1903-1990
> recalling life in the USSR in the 1930's

❖  ❖  ❖

## THE FELLOWSHIP OF THE GOSPEL—ROMANS 15:14-16:27

PAUL EXPLAINS TO THE Roman church the pioneering ministry to
which God has called him—Romans 15:14-21

But these admonitions are not because I have any doubts
about you, my dear friends. No, I am convinced that,
quite apart from me, you are outstanding in virtue,
advanced in knowledge and effective in ministering to one
another. True, I have expressed myself rather strongly in
part of this letter, but only to remind you of things you
already knew anyway. My boldness comes from the privilege given me by God to be a minister of Christ Jesus to
the Gentiles, serving in the holy ministry of the gospel of
God. It is the gospel that will make my offering of Gentile
converts well pleasing to God, sanctified by the Holy
Spirit. You see, then, why I take pride in my ministry—a
pride in Christ Jesus for what has been accomplished for
God. For I would not dare to claim any achievements
except what Christ has accomplished through me toward
the goal of winning obedience from the Gentiles. He is at
work through my speech and my life, by the miraculous
power of signs and wonders, by the power of the Holy
Spirit. It is by his power that I have fulfilled a ministry of
proclaiming the gospel from Jerusalem all the way to
Illyricum. But I have much more to do. And this is the

ministry I eagerly pursue: not to preach the gospel where
people have already bowed to Christ as Lord, but to take
it where he is not yet honored. I must not build my ministry on a foundation someone else has laid. Rather, God
has called me to the kind of missionary work described
by this biblical phrase:

> *They who had not been told of him before will*
> *see him,*
> *and they who had not heard of him before will*
> *know him.*

—Romans 15:14-21

**PRAYER**    O Lord God, we modern Christians can be so self-
absorbed. We look with condescension and boredom on the
missionary enterprise—when we think of it at all. God, forgive
us. We worship your Son in church on Sunday morning, we sing
our choruses with a euphoric joy, and we think we have honored him. But what do we know of honoring Christ, when we
remain content to let whole nations and peoples and tribes
around the world live and die without ever bowing to the One
whose name is above every other name? We have privatized our
faith. We have trivialized it as a merely personal benefit, like a
favorite television show or a hobby. We do not hear the gospel
as a war cry, as a summons to risk-taking, as a command to see
the Lord Jesus Christ honored in our own hearts as we exert
ourselves toward his being honored in others' hearts. O God,
your gospel spawns missionary effort as the sun radiates light.
The two are always found together. What then does our lack of
interest in missions reveal about our grasp of and love for the
gospel? O Lord, give fresh power to the gospel among *us.*
Revive in us the passion for Christian missions that thrust St.
Patrick and William Carey and David Livingstone and Hudson
Taylor and Amy Carmichael and thousands of others out to

the four winds, for the honor and glory of the Son of God. Dear Lord, deliver us from our convenience Christianity and lift us up to the infinite joy of kingdom-advancing missionary Christianity. In the holy name of Christ. Amen.

> *You wonder why people choose fields away from the States when young people at home are drifting because no one wants to take time to listen to their problems. I'll tell you why I left. Because those Stateside young people have every opportunity to study, hear and understand the Word of God in their own language, and these Indians have no opportunity whatsoever. I have had to make a cross of two logs, and lie down on it, to show the Indians what it means to crucify a man. When there is that much ignorance over here and so much knowledge and opportunity over there, I have no question in my mind why God sent me here. Those whimpering Stateside young people will wake up on the Day of Judgment condemned to worse fates than these demon-fearing Indians, because, having a Bible, they were bored with it, while these never heard of such a thing as writing.*

> *God, I pray Thee, light these idle sticks of my life and may I burn for Thee. Consume my life, my God, for it is Thine. I seek not a long life, but a full one, like you, Lord Jesus.*

> > *Jim Elliot, 1951, 1948*

✧   ✧   ✧

PAUL ENLISTS THE ROMAN church's support and prayers for his ministry—Romans 15:22-33

> The only reason, then, why I have been prevented from visiting you these many times is my demanding ministry to others who have not yet heard the gospel. But I have

now run out of fresh opportunities here in this area and have for many years wanted to visit you on my way to Spain. I would love to see you as I travel there and I hope that you will help me on my way, after I enjoy a little of your fellowship. But first, I am soon to leave for Jerusalem to help the Jewish believers there. For the churches here in Macedonia and Achaia have gladly contributed to the relief of the poor among God's people in Jerusalem. They have been happy to help, and so they should. Gentile believers owe a debt to Jewish believers. For if the Gentiles now share in the Jews' spiritual riches, it is only right that they minister back to them with material riches. So then, after I have fulfilled this responsibility and formalized the proper arrangements for their generous gift, I will leave for Spain, with you on my itinerary. And I am confident that, when I arrive, I will come laden with an abundance of blessing from Christ. But I want to press upon you, dear friends, given all that our Lord Jesus Christ means to us and given the love which the Spirit spreads among us, that you fight the battle at my side by praying to God for me. Pray in particular that I will be kept safe from those in Judea who reject the gospel. Pray also that this service I am performing—taking the Gentile donations to Jerusalem—will prove to be acceptable to them there. Then, God willing, I will come to you with joy and be refreshed in your company. Now may the God of peace be with you all. Amen.—Romans 15:22-33

**PRAYER**     O Chief Shepherd, you, above all, know the isolation of pastoral ministry. You understand the desolation a minister can suffer when he has no one to bear the burden with him. And you yourself, during your earthly sojourn, sincerely cared for the comfort of human fellow-feeling and the earnest prayers of friends. You prompted Paul to lay the Romans under a solemn and holy obligation not to abandon him to fend for himself but to support him and stand with him and pray him through his misgivings and adversities. O Lord of the Church, pour out upon your people today a spirit of supplication for your ministers. They bear a heavy burden under any conditions, but especially today. They are overworked, underpaid, disrespected, exploited. They are under sharp attack from the evil one. Many of them stand alone, when their churches ought to be gathering around, not with slavish flattery, but with sincere and strenuous intercession. If you would grant this request alone, dear Lord, what renewal would spread throughout your church in this generation! O Jesus, remember your ministers. In your holy name. Amen.

*O, it is at a fearful expense that ministers are ever allowed to enter the pulpit without being preceded, accompanied and followed by the earnest prayers of the churches. It is no marvel that the pulpit is so powerless and ministers so often disheartened when there are so few to hold up their hands. The consequence of neglecting this duty is seen and felt in the spiritual declension of the churches, and it will be seen and felt in the everlasting perdition of men, while the consequence of regarding it would be the ingathering of multitudes into the kingdom of God and new glories to the Lamb that was slain! . . . O, you blood-bought churches, your ministers need your prayers!*

*Gardiner Spring, 1848*

# ROMANS

## CHAPTER 16

PAUL INTRODUCES PHOEBE, who will carry his letter to Rome, and greets his friends in the church there—Romans 16:1-16

Now I commend to you Phoebe, our sister, who serves the church in Cenchrea. Please give her a Christian welcome worthy of God's people. Help her in any way she may need you, for she has herself befriended many, myself included. Please greet for me—

Priscilla and Aquila, my co-workers in Christ Jesus. They risked their lives to save mine. And I am not alone in my gratitude for them. All the Gentile churches feel this way. Greet also the church that meets in their house.

Epenetus, my dear friend, the first of the Asian harvest for Christ.

Mary, who has worked hard for you.

Andronicus and Junias, my relatives, who sat in prison with me. They are outstanding among the apostles, and converted to Christ before I did.

Ampliatus, my dear friend in the Lord.

Urbanus, our co-worker in Christ, and Stachys, my dear friend.

Apelles, a proven man of God.

Everyone in the household of Aristobulus.

Herodion, my relative.

The Christians in the household of Narcissus.

Tryphena and Tryphosa, who work hard for the Lord.

Persis, a dear friend, who has done so much work for the Lord.

Rufus, the Lord's chosen one, along with his mother, who has been a mother to me as well.

Asyncritus, Phlegon, Hermes, Patrobas, Hermas and the brothers with them.

Philologos and Julia, Nereus and his sister, and Olympas and all the saints with them.

Greet one another with a holy kiss. All the churches of Christ here send their greetings to you.—Romans 16:1-16

**PRAYER**   As I read, dear Lord, the names of your people in Rome, I see real people in all their life and warmth—Mary and Urbanus and Persis and the others, most of them ordinary people, like me. I see them as they gather in a Roman home for worship. They exchange greetings, smile, pray, sing, read a chapter of Paul's letter, discuss it together, meet you at your table, weep, laugh, bid one another farewell and go their separate ways back into the busy streets of Rome. I see them laboring, suffering, going to prison, sealing their testimony to you with their very blood. And their great accomplishments arose more out of great courage than great talent. Your grace flowed imperceptibly (even at times to them) but effectually through their praying and their thinking and their struggling each day, as you built your church. Their efforts must not have seemed glamorous most of the time. But you were there, present among your people, imparting to them the graces, virtues and victories that make a common life uncommonly significant.

Lord, the very fact that they were no different from me makes them all the more challenging to me. They are among that great cloud of witnesses whose lives insist upon the sufficiency of your grace for my weakness. They rose to the challenge of their historical situation. They did not give up and give in. O dear Lord, do not let me fail you today. Do not let me squander the hard-won gains handed down to me by previous generations of your church. Build your people today into a hard-working, risk-taking, joyfully uncompromising church laying a firm foundation for tomorrow. Let us be a strong link in the chain of your historic people. Let your church be stronger, not weaker, the day we die than it was the day we were born. Let the network of bold Christian collaboration spread widely, rapidly and effectively throughout our land and around the world through our efforts. O Lord, make us brave soldiers of the cross. In your holy name. Amen.

> *Am I a soldier of the cross,*
> *A follower of the Lamb?*
> *And shall I fear to own his cause,*
> *Or blush to speak his name?*

> *Must I be carried to the skies*
> *On flowery beds of ease,*
> *While others fought to win the prize*
> *And sailed through bloody seas?*

*Sure I must fight, if I would reign;*
*Increase my courage, Lord.*
*I'll bear the toil, endure the pain,*
*Supported by thy Word.*

*Isaac Watts, 1674–1748*

❖   ❖   ❖

PAUL ADDS A BRIEF warning against false teachers
—Romans 16:17-20

I urge you, dear friends, to be on your guard against those who would fragment the church and hinder your progress by introducing ideas contrary to the doctrine you have learned. See them for the danger they are and avoid them. Rather than serving our Lord Christ, such people are slaves to the gnawing demands of self. With attractive arguments and appeals to ego they deceive gullible people. No doubt they will target you, since your obedience has been so widely reported. And I am thrilled to hear good news about you. But I only want you to be deeply astute in all that is good and wholly pure of all that is evil. And the God of peace will soon crush Satan under your feet. The grace of our Lord Jesus be with you.—Romans 16:17-20

PRAYER    O Lord, how solemn a responsibility we who teach your church bear before you. Our impeccable credentials offer no protection from our selling and profaning your holy gospel. The fact that your people trust us only means that we have ample opportunity to gratify ego and greed through avenues of ministry. O Lord above, preserve us, both those who teach and those who are taught, from the lies of tongue and pen, from the bargain rates of consumer religion, from the vulgar empires of self-display. Let Holy Office truly be an outlet for service, never an opportunity for self. Raise up shepherds for your church who will sincerely care for your flock and who will faithfully lead them into the green pastures of the gospel as you have revealed it, not as popular trends would rewrite it. O Christ, keep your church wide awake to the false doctrine—so charming, so destructive—insinuating itself into our midst today, and preserve our confidence in the power of the true gospel. In your holy name. Amen.

> *From all evil and mischief, from sin, from the crafts and assaults*
> *of the devil, from thy wrath and from everlasting damnation,*
>   *Good Lord, deliver us.*
> *From all blindness of heart, from pride, vainglory and hypocrisy,*
> *from envy, hatred and malice and all uncharitableness,*
>   *Good Lord, deliver us. . . .*
> *From all false doctrine and heresy, from hardness of heart*
> *and contempt of thy Word and Commandment,*
>   *Good Lord, deliver us.*

The Second Prayer Book of Edward VI, *1552*

✧ ✧ ✧

PAUL CONCLUDES WITH final greetings and a benediction
—Romans 16:21-27

Timothy my co-worker sends his greetings, as do Lucius, Jason and Sosipater, my relatives. (I, Tertius, the one taking this letter down for Paul, greet you in the Lord.) Gaius, my host—in fact, he opens his home to the whole church here—greets you. Erastus, the city treasurer, and brother Quartus greet you.

Now all glory to the One who can make you strong, as my gospel, the message about Jesus Christ, declares. This message reveals what God had kept secret in timeless eternity but has now thrown open to the world. It is being made known, through the prophetic Scriptures, by command of the eternal God, so that all the nations may come to the obedience of faith. To the only wise God be glory forever through Jesus Christ! Amen.—Romans 16:21-27

**PRAYER**    Almighty God, most merciful Father, you are able to keep us in your grace. The encircling masses of our enemies—the thought police of secularism, the seductive sirens of hedonism, the salesmen of designer doctrine, as well as our own folly and sin—they cannot separate us from your saving love, for you are able to keep us against the complex devices of evil.

You do so through your gospel, which works in us with your power for our salvation. The gospel, concealed so long, promised so long, proclaimed at last—the gospel, my sweet and solemn pleasure, the infinitely precious gospel of the Lord Jesus Christ—this is our dearest treasure in life. Burn down the Sistine Chapel, and we are very much the poorer. Kill our children, and we are heartbroken. Take away your gospel, *and we are lost!* But renew in us a loving fascination with, a confident belief in, and a deep understanding of your gospel, *and we seize life!* O God, for the gospel let me live and let me die. In the holy name of Christ. Amen.

> O *what amazing words of grace,*
>   *Are in the gospel found,*
> *Suited to every sinner's case*
>   *Who knows the joyful sound.*

> *Poor, sinful, thirsty, fainting souls*
>   *Are freely welcome here.*
> *Salvation like a river rolls*
>   *Abundant, free and clear.*

*Come, then, with all your wants and wounds,*
  *Your every burden bring.*
*Here love, unchanging love, abounds,*
  *A deep, celestial spring.*

*Millions of sinners, vile as you,*
  *Have found here life and peace!*
*Come then and prove its virtues too,*
  *And drink, adore and bless.*

*Samuel Medley, 1738–1799*

# AFTERWORD

## AN EARNEST CALL FOR EVANGELICAL LEADERS TO RECOVER THE GOSPEL FROM ITS PRESENT HUMILIATION

A WAVE OF AUTHENTIC REVIVAL sweeps over the church when three things happen together: teaching the great truths of the gospel with clarity, applying those truths to people's lives with spiritual power, and extending that experience to large numbers of people.[1] We evangelicals urgently need such an awakening today. We need to rediscover the gospel.

Imagine the evangelical church without the gospel. I know this makes no sense, for evangelicals are *defined* by the evangel. But try to imagine it for just a moment. What might our evangelicalism, without the evangel, look like? We would have to replace the centrality of the gospel with something else, naturally. So what might take the place of the gospel in our sermons and books and cassette tapes and Sunday school classes and home Bible studies and, above all, in our hearts? A number of things, conceivably. An introspective absorption with recovery from past emotional traumas, for example. Or a passionate devotion to the pro-life cause. Or a confident manipulation of modern managerial techniques. Or a drive toward church growth and "success." Or a deep concern for the institution of the family. Or a fascination with the more unusual gifts of the Spirit. Or a clever appeal to consumerism by offering a sort of cost-free Christianity Lite. Or a sympathetic, empathetic, thickly-honeyed cultivation of interpersonal relationships. Or a determination to take America back to its Christian roots through political power. Or a warm affirmation of self-esteem. The evangelical movement, stripped of the gospel, might fix upon any or several of such concerns to define itself and derive energy for its mission. In other words, evangelicals could marginalize or even lose the gospel and still potter on their way, perhaps even oblivious to their loss.

But not only is this conceivable, it is actually happening among us right now. Whatever one may think of the various concerns noted above as alternatives to the centrality of the gospel—and some of these matters possess genuine validity and even urgency, especially the family—not one of them is *central* to our faith. Not one of them *is* the gospel or deserves to push the gospel itself to the periphery of our message, our agenda and our affections. But the gospel of our blessed Lord Jesus Christ is today suffering humiliation among us evangelicals by our conspicuous neglect of it.

When we think of the gospel, we may have a feeling that "We already know that. Ho-hum." We assume the gospel as a given. We assume that the people in our churches know the gospel, and we are anxious to move on to more "relevant" and "practical" topics. The gospel is being set aside in our minds and hearts in favor of a broad range of issues, as broadly ranging as evangelicalism is fragmented, while the heart and soul of our faith is falling into obscurity through neglect. The holy mysteries of the incarnation, cross, resurrection, ascension and heavenly reign of our Lord, the great themes of election, propitiation, justification and sanctification, the power and deceitfulness of sin, the meaning of faith and repentance, our union with our crucified, buried and risen Lord, the infinitely superior value of our heavenly reward compared with anything this life has to offer (including the Christian life), the final judgment and eternity—these glorious themes which lie at the very center of our faith, which made the church great at her greatest moments in the past and which can do the same again for us today if only we will recover them and exploit them confidently, prayerfully and biblically, these

infinitely precious treasures are being bypassed in favor of legitimate but secondary matters of concern. We must guard the centrality of that which is central.

We should not think, "Well, of course we have the gospel. The
Reformation recovered it for us." Such complacency will cost us
dearly. Every generation of Christians must be retaught afresh the
basic truths of our faith. The church is always one generation
away from total ignorance of the gospel, and we today are making rapid progress toward that ruinous goal. *Rather than care-
lessly assume the gospel, we must aggressively, deliberately, fully
and passionately teach and preach the gospel.* All the treasures
of wisdom and knowledge are *hidden* in Christ. If we do not
intentionally search them out, we will miss them.

Pastors and church leaders, in particular, are under enormous
pressure today to satisfy the immediate demands of the market-
place at the cost of the gospel. People want what they want when
they want it, or they will drive down the street to the First Church
of Where-It's-At to get it. Are we leaders losing our nerve? Have
we come to feel that the gospel itself meets people's needs less
convincingly and helpfully? But think about it. Without a clear
understanding of the central truths of our faith, where will the
wisdom and motivation to live godly lives come from? We are
constantly offering people "Five Steps to (whatever)" in answer
to their problems. But it is not working. To a shameful degree,
we Christians are morally indistinct from the world. Why? One
reason is that we think piecemeal, and our lives show it. We do
not perceive reality from God's perspective. We perceive reality
from the perspective of our ungodly culture, and then we try to
slap a biblical principle onto the surface of our deep confusion.
Consequently, very little actually changes. What we really need
is not to be pandered to but to be re-educated in reality, as it is
interpreted for us by the gospel. We need to know who God
really is. We need to find out who we really are. We need to
understand what our root problem really is and what God's mer-

ciful answer really is. And we need that new perception of reality to percolate deep down into our affections and desires, reorienting us radically and joyfully to a whole new way of life. But if we frankly feel that the plain old gospel offers very little for people's real needs, then we have never really known it at all.

We evangelicals today are suffering massive defeat, brilliantly disguised as massive success. A record high 74% of Americans eighteen years of age and older say they have made a commitment to Jesus Christ, according to a recent Gallup Poll. That could suggest a high degree of effectiveness in our witness. But at the same time—as if we needed verification of the fact—a survey by the Roper Organization shows little difference in the moral behavior of "born-again" Christians before and after their conversion.[2] If we come under the spell of ratings appeal rather than the imperatives of the gospel, what room can there be for the narrow gate and the hard way? Even as our churches enjoy a measure of outward success, we remain the influenced, not the influential, as long as we shift our power-base from the ways of God to the ways of man, from Spirit-anointed biblical truth to human skills and novelties. Operating in a man-centered rather than a God-centered mode, our churches do not necessarily fail. They stand as good a chance of success as any other franchise network. Some even become popular—but popular *as what*? As a religious pastime, or as a force for God?

> *And you, O desolate one,*
> *what do you mean that you dress in scarlet,*
>    *that you deck yourself with ornaments of gold,*
>       *that you enlarge your eyes with paint?*
> *In vain you beautify yourself.*
>    *Your lovers despise you;*
>    *they seek your life.*

—Jeremiah 4:30

O desolate evangelicalism, what do you mean by your stylish fads and restless search for ever new "relevance"? Why are you so insecure that you long for the world's approving recognition? They despise everything you hold dear! "All things to all men" is no license to cater to the whims of the consumer. Christ alone is Lord. Or have you yourself forgotten his majesty? And why are you so boastful of your numbers and dollars? How poor you really are! Come back to the gospel. Come back to the wellspring of true joy and life and power. Sanctify Christ again as Lord in your hearts. Wake up! Strengthen what remains, for it is on the point of death. But if you will *not* return to the centrality of the gospel as God's power for the church today, then what reason does your Lord have for not abandoning you altogether?

# LIST OF SOURCES QUOTED

TO ALLOW READERS TO EXPLORE FURTHER THE
SOURCES I HAVE DRAWN UPON IN THE COURSE OF
THIS BOOK, I LIST THEM HERE:

Romans 1:1 *The Church Hymnary: Revised Edition* (London: Oxford University Press, 1927), #518.

Romans 1:2 Alexander Solzhenitsyn, *'One Word of Truth . . .'* (London: The Bodley Head, 1972), page 27.

Romans 1:3-4 *The Book of Common Prayer* (New York: The Church Pension Fund, 1945), page 10.

Romans 1:5-6 Harold J. Ockenga, *The Church God Blesses* (Pasadena: Fuller Missions Fellowship and Board of Missions, Park Street Church, 1959), page 35.

Romans 1:7 Anselm, *Proslogion,* in Eugene R. Fairweather, editor and translator, *A Scholastic Miscellany: Anselm to Ockham* (Philadelphia: The Westminster Press, 1956), page 79.

Romans 1:8-10 *The Works of Jonathan Edwards* (Edinburgh: The Banner of Truth Trust, 1979), II:292.

Romans 1:11-15 *Christianity Today,* 20 June 1960, page 6.

Romans 1:16-17 Ned Bernard Stonehouse, editor, *God Transcendent: Messages by J. Gresham Machen* (Edinburgh: The Banner of Truth Trust, 1982), pages 89f.

Roland Bainton, *Here I Stand: A Life of Martin Luther* (New York: Abingdon-Cokesbury, 1950), page 65. Cf. *Eerdmans' Handbook to the History of Christianity* (Grand Rapids: Wm. B. Eerdmans Company, 1977), page 366.

Romans 1:18 Whittaker Chambers, *Witness* (New York: Random House, 1952), page 16.

Romans 1:19-20 *The Works of John Dryden: Poems, 1685-1692* (Berkeley: University of California Press, 1969), III: 201.

Philip Schaff, editor, *The Creeds of Christendom* (Grand Rapids: Baker Book House, 1990), III:384.

Romans 1:21-23 Anselm, *Proslogion,* in Eugene R. Fairweather, editor and translator, *A Scholastic Miscellany: Anselm to Ockham* (Philadelphia: The Westminster Press, 1956), page 86.

Romans 1:24-25 Jeremiah Burroughs, *A Treatise of Earthly-Mindedness* (Ligonier, Pennsylvania: Soli Deo Gloria, 1991), page 18.

Romans 1:26-27 Jean Hagstrum and James Gray, editors, *Samuel Johnson: Sermons* (New Haven and London: Yale University Press, 1978), pages 215-218.

Romans 1:28-32 Augustine, *Confessions*, Book I, Chapter 5.

Romans 2:1 J. C. Ryle, *Old Paths, being Plain Statements on Some of the Weightier Matters of Christianity* (London: James Clarke, 1972), page 130, footnote 2.

Romans 2:2-4 *The Church Hymnary: Revised Edition* (London: Oxford University Press, 1927), #408.

Romans 2:5 *The Church Hymnary: Revised Edition* (London: Oxford University Press, 1927), #405.

Romans 2:6-11 Tom Ingram and Douglas Newton, *Hymns as Poetry* (London: Constable and Company, 1956), page 241.

Romans 2:12-13 William Law, *A Serious Call to a Holy and Devout Life*, edited by John W. Meister and others (Philadelphia: The Westminster Press, 1955), pages 19f.

Romans 2:14-16 *The Church Hymnary: Revised Edition* (London: Oxford University Press, 1927), #161.

Romans 2:17-24 William B. Sprague, *Lectures on Revivals of Religion* (Edinburgh: The Banner of Truth Trust, 1978), pages 86f.

Romans 2:25-29 *The Church Hymnary: Revised Edition* (London: Oxford University Press, 1927), #191.

Romans 3:1-4 *The Revival of Religion: Addresses by Scottish Evangelical Leaders delivered in Glasgow in 1840* (Edinburgh: The Banner of Truth Trust, 1984), pages 315ff.

Romans 3:5-8 *Sermons of Robert Murray McCheyne* (Edinburgh: The Banner of Truth Trust, 1972), pages 177f.

Romans 3:9-20 *Grace Hymns*, second edition (London: Grace Publications Trust, 1984), #699.

Romans 3:21-26 William Gadsby, *A Selection of Hymns for Public Worship* (Harpenden, England: Gospel Standard Strict Baptist Trust, Ltd., 1978), #227.

John Bunyan, *The Pilgrim's Progress From This World to That Which is To Come* (New York: Fleming H. Revell Company, 1903), pages 45f.

Romans 3:27-31 *The Works of Jonathan Edwards* (Edinburgh: The Banner of Truth Trust, 1979), I:398f.

Romans 4:1-8 *Grace Hymns*, second edition (London: Grace Publications Trust, 1984), #388.

Romans 4:9-12 John Pollock, *George Whitefield and the Great Awakening* (Garden City, New York: Doubleday & Company, Inc., 1972), page 244.

Romans 4:13-17a *The Works of Richard Sibbes* (Edinburgh: The Banner of Truth Trust, 1983), VI:21.

Romans 4:17b-22 John Calvin, *The Epistles of Paul the Apostle to the Romans and to the Thessalonians*, translated by Ross MacKenzie (Grand Rapids: Wm. B. Eerdmans Company, 1980), page 99.

Romans 4:23-25 *The Methodist Hymnal* (New York: Easton & Mains, 1905), #297.

Romans 5:1-5 *Sermons of Robert Murray McCheyne* (Edinburgh: The Banner of Truth Trust, 1972), pages 124f.

Romans 5:6-10 John N. Wall, Jr., editor, *George Herbert: The Country Parson, The Temple* (New York: The Paulist Press, 1981), page 316.

Romans 5:11 William Gadsby, *A Selection of Hymns for Public Worship* (Harpenden, England: Gospel Standard Strict Baptist Trust, Ltd., 1978), #185.

Romans 5:12-14a Anselm, *Proslogion*, in Eugene R. Fairweather, editor and translator, *A Scholastic Miscellany: Anselm to Ockham* (Philadelphia: The Westminster Press, 1956), pages 85f.

Romans 5:14b-17 Ned Bernard Stonehouse, editor, *God Transcendent: Messages by J. Gresham Machen* (Edinburgh: The Banner of Truth Trust, 1982), pages 189f.

Romans 5:18-21 Peter C. Rae, "Joseph Hart and His Hymns," *Scottish Bulletin of Evangelical Theology* 6 (1988): 22f.

Romans 6:1-5 H. C. G. Moule, *The Epistle to the Romans* (London: Pickering & Inglis, Ltd., n.d.), pages 159-161.

Romans 6:6-11 Tom Ingram and Douglas Newton, *Hymns as Poetry* (London: Constable and Company, 1956), pages 266f.

Romans 6:12-14 Dietrich Bonhoeffer, *The Cost of Discipleship* (New York: The Macmillan Company, 1959), pages 35f.

Romans 6:15-17 Thomas Brooks, *Precious Remedies Against Satan's Devices* (Edinburgh: The Banner of Truth Trust, 1990), page 32.

Romans 6:18-23 *The Letters of Samuel Rutherford* (Edinburgh: Oliphant, Anderson & Ferrier, 1891), #CCLXXXIII.

Romans 7:1-4 Thomas Brooks, *Precious Remedies Against Satan's Devices* (Edinburgh: The Banner of Truth Trust, 1990), pages 123f.

Romans 7:5-6 *Grace Hymns*, second edition (London: Grace Publications Trust, 1984), #647.

Romans 7:7-12 *The Confession of Faith; The Larger and Shorter Catechisms* (Edinburgh: Free Presbyterian Church of Scotland, 1976), pages 236f.

William Gadsby, *A Selection of Hymns for Public Worship* (Harpenden, England: Gospel Standard Strict Baptist Trust, Ltd., 1978), #46.

Romans 7:13-14 *Selections from Cowper's Poems* (London: Macmillan and Company, 1912), page 159.

Romans 7:15-25 *The Works of John Newton* (Edinburgh: The Banner of Truth Trust, 1985), III:607f.

Romans 8:1-4 Henry Scougal, *The Life of God in the Soul of Man* (London: InterVarsity Fellowship, 1967), pages 15f.

Romans 8:5-8 Malcolm Muggeridge, *Like It Was: The Diaries of Malcolm Muggeridge* (London: Collins, 1981), page 434.

Romans 8:9-11 *Grace Hymns*, second edition (London: Grace Publications Trust, 1984), #332.

Romans 8:12-14 John Owen, *Sin & Temptation: The Challenge To Personal Godliness*, abridged and edited by James M. Houston (Portland: Multnomah Press, 1983), pages 166f.

Romans 8:15-17 *The Preces Privatae of Lancelot Andrewes, Bishop of Winchester*, translated by F. E. Brightman (London: Methuen & Co., 1903), page 192.

Romans 8:18-21 Tom Ingram and Douglas Newton, *Hymns as Poetry* (London: Constable and Company, 1956), pages 200f.

Romans 8:22-25 Anselm, *Proslogion*, in Eugene R. Fairweather, editor and translator, *A Scholastic Miscellany: Anselm to Ockham* (Philadelphia: The Westminster Press, 1956), pages 92f.

Romans 8:26-30 *Selections from Cowper's Poems* (London: Macmillan and Company, 1912), page 158.

Romans 8:31-37 Jock Purves, *Fair Sunshine: Character Studies of the Scottish Covenanters* (Edinburgh: The Banner of Truth Trust, 1990), pages 92f.

Romans 8:38-39 Charles Erlandson, editor, *Charles H. Spurgeon: The Best from All His Works* (Nashville: Thomas Nelson, 1988), page 266.

Romans 9:1-5 John Bunyan, *The Pilgrim's Progress From This World to That Which is To Come* (New York: Fleming H. Revell Company, 1903), page 170.

Romans 9:6-9 Martyn Lloyd-Jones, *Revival* (Westchester, Illinois: Crossway Books, 1987), page 300.

Romans 9:10-13 William Gadsby, *A Selection of Hymns for Public Worship* (Harpenden, England: Gospel Standard Strict Baptist Trust, Ltd., 1978), #4.

Romans 9:14-18 *The Works of Jonathan Edwards* (Edinburgh: The Banner of Truth Trust, 1979), I:xiif.

Romans 9:19-21 C. S. Lewis, *Mere Christianity* (New York: The Macmillan Company, 1958), page 113.

Romans 9:22-23 Charles Haddon Spurgeon, "The Comfort of Sovereignty," *Tabletalk*, November, 1992, pages 13f.

Romans 9:24-29 William Gadsby, *A Selection of Hymns for Public Worship* (Harpenden, England: Gospel Standard Strict Baptist Trust, Ltd., 1978), #690.

Romans 9:30-33 H. C. G. Moule, *The Epistle to the Romans* (London: Pickering & Inglis, Ltd., n.d.), page 260.

Romans 10:1-4 Blaise Pascal, *Thoughts* (New York: P. F. Collier & Sons, 1910), page 274.

Horatius Bonar, *Words to Winners of Souls* (Garland, Texas: American Tract Society, 1981), reprint, page 11.

Romans 10:5-8 Thomas Brooks, *Precious Remedies Against Satan's Devices* (Edinburgh: The Banner of Truth Trust, 1990), page 141.

Romans 10:9 A personal statement.

Romans 10:10-13 C. S. Lewis, *The Weight of Glory and Other Addresses* (Grand Rapids: Wm. B. Eerdmans Company, 1974), pages 64f.

Romans 10:14-17 *The Confession of Faith; The Larger and Shorter Catechisms* (Edinburgh: Free Presbyterian Church of Scotland, 1976), page 253.

Romans 10:18-21 J. C. Ryle, *Holiness* (Old Tappan, New Jersey: Fleming H. Revell Company, n.d.), pages 238f.

Romans 11:1-6 *The Hymnal of the Protestant Episcopal Church* (New York: The Church Pension Fund, 1940), #405.

Romans 11:7-10 *The Revival of Religion: Addresses by Scottish Evangelical Leaders delivered in Glasgow in 1840* (Edinburgh: The Banner of Truth Trust, 1984), pages 383f.

Romans 11:11-16 *The Church Hymnary: Revised Edition* (London: Oxford University Press, 1927), #160.

Romans 11:17-24 Richard Hooker, "On the Certainty and Perpetuity of Faith in the Elect," in *Of the Laws of Ecclesiastical Polity* (London: J. M. Dent & Sons, Ltd., 1907), page 12.

Romans 11:25-32 *Donne's Sermons: Selected Passages* (Oxford: The Clarendon Press, 1932), pages 136ff.

Romans 11:33-36 *Grace Hymns*, second edition (London: Grace Publications Trust, 1984), #13.

Romans 12:1-2 *The Works of Jonathan Edwards* (Edinburgh: The Banner of Truth Trust, 1979), I:xxv.

Romans 12:3-8 *The Practical Works of Richard Baxter: A Christian Directory* (Ligonier, Pennsylvania: Soli Deo Gloria, 1990), page 201.

Romans 12:9-13 William Bradford, *Of Plymouth Plantation*, edited by Samuel Eliot Morison (New York: Alfred A. Knopf, 1953), pages 77f.

Romans 12:14-21 *The Church Hymnary: Revised Edition* (London: Oxford University Press, 1927), #520.

Romans 13:1-7 Roland Bainton, *Here I Stand: A Life of Martin Luther* (New York: Abingdon-Cokesbury, 1950), page 174.

Romans 13:8-10 *The Church Hymnary: Revised Edition* (London: Oxford University Press, 1927), #492.

Romans 13:11-14 J. C. Ryle, *Holiness* (Old Tappan, New Jersey: Fleming H. Revell Company, n.d.), page 64.

Romans 14:1-12 *The Works of Richard Sibbes* (Edinburgh: The Banner of Truth Trust, 1978), V:305.

Romans 14:13-23 Roland Bainton, *Here I Stand: A Life of Martin Luther* (New York: Abingdon-Cokesbury, 1950), page 185. Cf. *Eerdmans' Handbook to the History of Christianity* (Grand Rapids: Wm. B. Eerdmans Company, 1977), page 364.

Romans 15:1-6 Francis Schaeffer, *Two Contents, Two Realities*, in *The Complete Works of Francis Schaeffer* (Westchester, Illinois: Crossway Books, 1986), III:419ff.

Romans 15:7-12 William Gadsby, *A Selection of Hymns for Public Worship* (Harpenden, England: Gospel Standard Strict Baptist Trust, Ltd., 1978), #816.

Romans 15:13 Malcolm Muggeridge, *Chronicles of Wasted Time, Chronicle 1: The Green Stick* (New York: Quill, 1982), pages 258f.

Romans 15:14-21 Elisabeth Elliot, *Shadow of the Almighty: The Life & Testament of Jim Elliot* (New York: Harper & Brothers, 1958), pages 237, 247.

Romans 15:22-33 Gardiner Spring, *A Plea to Pray for Pastors* (Amityville, New York: Calvary Press, 1991), pages 5ff.

Romans 16:1-16 *Worship and Service Hymnal* (Carol Stream, Illinois: Hope Publishing Company, 1975), #457.

Romans 16:17-20 *The First and Second Prayer Books of Edward VI* (London: J. M. Dent & Sons, Ltd., 1957), pages 361f.

Romans 16:21-27 *Grace Hymns*, second edition (London: Grace Publications Trust, 1984), #363.

# ENDNOTES

### Foreword

1. Frederick L. Godet, *Commentary on St. Paul's Epistle to the Romans* (Edinburgh: T. & T. Clark, 1886), page viii.
2. *Ibid.*, page 1.

### Preface

1. Thomas Watson, *The Ten Commandments* (Edinburgh: The Banner of Truth Trust, 1981), page 6.
2. Thomas Scott, *The Force of Truth* (Edinburgh: The Banner of Truth Trust, 1984), pages 122f.

### Introduction

1. I owe a special debt to the commentaries of Charles Hodge (1886), H. C. G. Moule (1893), C. E. B. Cranfield (1975, 1979) and Leon Morris (1988). I was much influenced in my interpretation of chapter nine by John Piper's *The Justification of God* (1983).

### Afterword

1. I am grateful to my friend and colleague, Dr. Tom Nettles, for suggesting this to me.
2. *National and International Religion Report*, 8 October 1990, page 8.

# NOTES AND PRAYERS